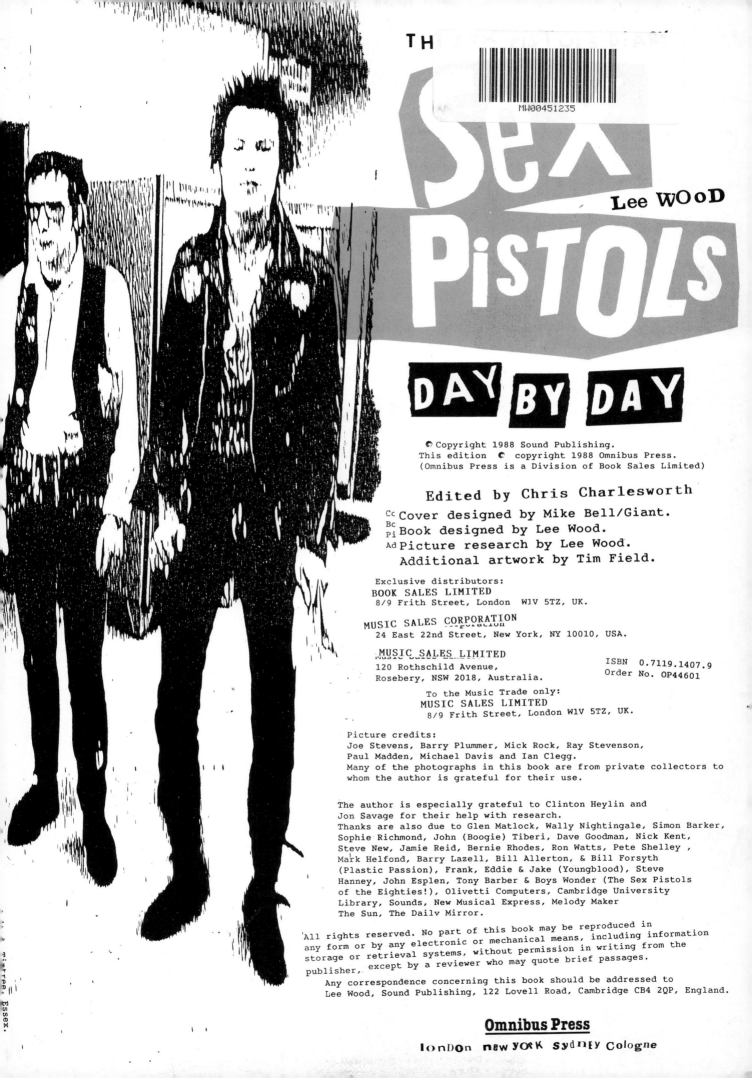

THE Sex PiSTOLS

Lee WOoD

DAY BY DAY

Edited by Chris Charlesworth

Cover designed by Mike Bell/Giant.
Book designed by Lee Wood.
Picture research by Lee Wood.
Additional artwork by Tim Field.

Exclusive distributors:
BOOK SALES LIMITED
8/9 Frith Street, London W1V 5TZ, UK.

MUSIC SALES CORPORATION
24 East 22nd Street, New York, NY 10010, USA.

MUSIC SALES LIMITED
120 Rothschild Avenue,
Rosebery, NSW 2018, Australia.

ISBN 0.7119.1407.9
Order No. OP44601

To the Music Trade only:
MUSIC SALES LIMITED
8/9 Frith Street, London W1V 5TZ, UK.

Picture credits:
Joe Stevens, Barry Plummer, Mick Rock, Ray Stevenson,
Paul Madden, Michael Davis and Ian Clegg.
Many of the photographs in this book are from private collectors to
whom the author is grateful for their use.

The author is especially grateful to Clinton Heylin and
Jon Savage for their help with research.
Thanks are also due to Glen Matlock, Wally Nightingale, Simon Barker,
Sophie Richmond, John (Boogie) Tiberi, Dave Goodman, Nick Kent,
Steve New, Jamie Reid, Bernie Rhodes, Ron Watts, Pete Shelley ,
Mark Helfond, Barry Lazell, Bill Allerton, & Bill Forsyth
(Plastic Passion), Frank, Eddie & Jake (Youngblood), Steve
Hanney, John Esplen, Tony Barber & Boys Wonder (The Sex Pistols
of the Eighties!), Olivetti Computers, Cambridge University
Library, Sounds, New Musical Express, Melody Maker
The Sun, The Daily Mirror.

Any correspondence concerning this book should be addressed to
Lee Wood, Sound Publishing, 122 Lovell Road, Cambridge CB4 2QP, England.

Omnibus Press

lonDon new YorK sydney Cologne

King's Road
and around
by VIVIEN GOLDSMITH

Rock—not so much a gimmick, more a way of life

FOR SOME, rock 'n roll is the latest gimmick t latch on to, but for others it's a way of life tha they never left.

A shop called Let It Rock, which is in King's Road, nea Moravian Corner, is run by someone who falls into the latte category.

Malcolm McLaren, who's aged 26, recently left Goldsmith's College, where he studied art. He was engaged on making a film about Oxford Street through the ages but it sort of got stuck in the 50s, and turned into a film about Billy Fury.

That is not to criticise him for having "got stuck" in the 50s—he feels at home in the period, so why follow current fashions for the sake of them. At the moment it looks like he's going to be bang up to date with the trends. Malcolm says he does not object to the "trendies" coming into his shop and picking up his style.

Style is something the rockers have got worked out. Let It Rock sells drapes—long jackets trimmed with velvet, made by Screaming Lord Sutch's tailor. A large proportion of their stock is genuine 1950s, but at the rate it's being snatched up, the stock will soon have to be entirely new.

Brocade waistcoats for boys and girls at £3.95 and "V"-necked Tee shirts for girls at £2.30 are very good value. Drapes cost about £25, which is much less than rockers have to pay to get them tailor-made.

CHICKEN BONES

A more unusual item of clothing which will soon be available in the shop is chicken-bone jackets. These are leather or suedette jackets with a pattern of real chicken bones on the outside.

To complete the 1950s scene there's guaranteed re-conditioned valve radios from £3, old film magazines, James Dean cinema stills and rock records.

The records cost from 15p to £2.50 for rare ones like Danny and the Juniors at the Hop. Most of the records come from dusty attics, but others were sent over direct from Memphis, Tennessee.

Malcolm hopes to be able to transfer the shop a few doors along to premises with a large basement, that could be converted into a coffee bar. This would then make Let It Rock a centre for people to meet and talk.

SITTING ROOM

They already try to give the shop a friendly atmosphere. There's a 50s-style sitting room at the back of the shop where people can sit and talk or just listen to the incredible sounds that come out of the juke-box.

On good days, Malcolm says that he sometimes buys cakes and Coke to give to his customers. He admitted that this was to appease his conscience. Thinking that "capitalism stinks," he has doubts about running the shop.

He wants to earn enough money from the enterprise to be able to finish his film, which he had to give up for lack of funds.

He also feels that the shop fulfils a need for rockers: they come to it from miles around.

It is the first shop to sell exclusive rocker gear. In the 1950s it was not considered respectable to buy drapes off the peg, even if they were made, which they weren't. Back-street tailors and Burtons got their custom, and the rest of their gear was bought from ordinary shops.

At the moment the shop is a rocker oasis in a hip world, but soon it may not be distinguishable to the passer-by from the trendy imitations that are bound to spring up around it in King's Road.

Anyone who ventures inside will be struck by the genuine passion that Malcolm and his assistant Bill Hegarty have for all the things they sell. It is so real, they admit that they don't like selling any of it—but they will.

MALCOLM MCLAREN pictured at the back of his King's Road shop. Let It Rock—a cosy 1950s sitting room hidden away from the sophisticated 'seventies. (King's Road and Around last week).

THE EARLY YEARS

1971

While still at school Paul Cook and Steve Jones would take days off and head for the home of Warwick (Wally) Nightingale where they would all spend the day sitting in the back garden, drinking cans of beer and listening to records. After finally leaving school they enjoyed getting drunk and going to concerts with a few friends including Jimmy Mackin, Stephen Hayes and a guy called Cecil. Meanwhile, Malcolm McLaren (whom they have yet to meet) is opening a shop called 'Let It Rock' at 430 Kings Road, Chelsea.

1972/1973

Wally tried to get them interested in playing music and suggested they should form a band as he could already play guitar. Paul scraped together some money and bought a secondhand set of Olympic drums and Steve decided to be the singer. Jimmy Mackin bought a Farfisa organ, Cecil acquired some Congos and Stephen Hayes was to be the bass player. Steve with the help of Wally started to steal items of musical equipment, mainly guitars and amplifiers which Wally then used. It was all so "hot" they couldn't risk selling it. Time passed, but Stephen and Jimmy never learnt to play their instruments, so Del Noone a relation of Paul's was brought in to play bass. Rehearsals started at 533 Kings Road. Wally made a recording of a rehearsal from this period but years later taped over it with a Pretenders album! Del, who was married to Paul's sister often failed to turn up at rehearsals, and soon stopped coming altogether. Cecil and his Congos never managed to be heard above the amplified noise and he also left.

FEB/MARCH 1973

Around this time Malcolm McLaren changed the name of his shop from "Let It Rock" to "Too Fast To Live, Too Young To Die".

MID 1973 ONWARDS

They already knew Malcolm McLaren because they were always hanging around the Kings Road area of Chelsea, and were constantly in and out of his shop.

LATE 1973

Malcolm seemed interested in what the band were doing and tried to help them. He had found them a rehearsal place in Covent Garden but the band didn't like it and only used it a few times. Glen Matlock worked in the shop on Saturdays and soon heard of the opening for a bass guitarist. One rehearsal held in Wally's bedroom where he played 'Three Button Hand Me Down' (The Faces) convinced them he was the person they had been looking for and he joined the band. With Glen in the band they had one final rehearsal in Covent Garden.

I DID YOU NO WRONG

I DON'T MIND THE THINGS YOU SAY.
I DON'T MIND GOING OUT OF MY WAY
TO TRY AND DO THINGS FOR YOU,
BUT IN RETURN I GET TREATED SO CRUEL

I HAD A MIND BENDING TRIP AROUND THE U.S.A.
RUNNING AFTER YOU TRYIN TO FIND A WAY.
TO BRING YOU BACK HOME WITH ME
GET YOU IN MY ARMS TRY AND MAKE YOU SEE,

THE THINGS I HEARD ABOUT *you* ME WERE LIES
REMEMBER I TOLD YOU ON THE NIGHT YOU CRIED
BUT YOU WOULDN'T HAVE IT FROM ME.
YOU HAD TO GO YOUR OWN WAY AND TAKE
YOUR KEY.

GUITAR BREAK

I GOT A GREAT BIG TRAVELING SHOW.
AND I SHURE WOULD LIKE YOU TO KNOW.
IF YOU'VE GOT NOWHERE TO GO.
COME WITH ME GIRL.

I GOT ONE BIG HELL OF A BAND.
AND I SHURE COULD DO WITH A HAND.
BUT IT'S UP TO YOU MY FRIEND.
YES ITS UP TO YOU.

WINDOW the metal window company ltd

CONTRACTORS TO MINISTRY OF PUBLIC BUILDING & WORKS & G.L.C.
METAL WINDOW REPAIR, FIXING & MAINTENANCE SPECIALISTS

MOZART HOUSE, LANDOR WALK, SHEPHERDS BUSH, W.12. 9AR

Tel. Nos: 01-749 3466
01-743 0963

DIRECTORS: C. W. IRVINE
J. B. IRVINE

Our Ref: CWI/DB

S. Jones Esq.,
40, Hegis House,
Sleaford Street,
London S.W.8.

26th February, 1974.

Dear Steve,

Please find enclosed Insurance Card, P.45 and wages due to date.

Yours sincerely,

p/ Bill.

SCARFACE:

NOW THERE WAS A BOY WITH A REAL CLEAN FACE
PLENTY OF BIRDS FROM PLACE TO PLACE
THEN ONE DAY HE CAME ON STRONG
THATS WHEN THINGS STARTED TO GO WRONG

CHORUS
SCARFACE SCARRED FROM EAR TO EAR
SCARFACE THE GIRLS DONT EVEN CARE

2 HE DRESSED UP WELL IN CLASSY GEAR
THE GIRLS WOULD PAY FOR THE CLOTHES HE'D WEAR
HE'D TELL THEM HE LOVED THEM BUT THAT WOULD BE A LIE
'COS WHEN HE'D USED THEM HE' JUST WAVE GOODBYE

CHORUS X 2   LEAD X 2   CHORUS X 1   VERSE (NO VOCAL DRUMS)

3 HE TOOK A MYSTERY TO A BAR ONE NIGHT
DIDN'T KNOW HER BOY FRIEND WAS IN SITE
PUT UP HIS HANDS AND FELT BLOOD ON HIS FACE
THATS HOW HE GOT HIS NAME SCARFACE

4 HE'S A LOSER NOW WITH AN UGLY FACE
NO MORE BIRDS AROUND THE PLACE
YOU'LL SEE HIM STANDING ON THE CORNER ON HIS OWN
MAYBE STILL DREAMING OF THE GIRLS HE'S KNOWN

CHORUS   FADE

(The above is a copy of the song 'SCARFACE' that THE SWANKERS played at rehearsals
and at their only live performance at Salters Cafe.   (c) 1973/4 Warwick Nightingale)

JANUARY 1974

Steve discovered a new place to rehearse called Shesuma, located in the basement of 90 Lots Road, London SW10.

FEBRUARY/MARCH 1974

Steve Jones leaves his job working for a double glazing company called "Window Conversion & Repair Co Ltd". He buys a motorbike registration number TYM 46M.

SUMMER 1974

Rehearsals now move to the long-vacated BBC TV Riverside studios in Hammersmith, available at no cost, thanks to Wally's dad, who ran his own electrical business and had been contracted to rewire the premises. The band had a set of keys cut and occupied what had been the film sound dubbing room, this was said to offer the best sound acoustics in Europe! These facilities were used for nearly a year, covering a selection of 60's songs by The Who and Small Faces, The Love Affair's 'A Day Without Love', The Foundations 'Build Me Up Buttercup' and The Rolling Stones 'It's All Over Now', plus two original songs called 'I Did You No Wrong' and 'Scarface'. 'Did You No Wrong' was written by Wally, Paul Cook wrote the original set of words. Most of these were later changed by Johnny Rotten when he joined. 'Scarface' was written by Wally and his dad. Through Malcolm they got to know Nick Kent a music journalist for New Musical Express. While they were rehearsing on a couple of occasions (probably on Saturday evenings after meeting in Malcolm's shop and a few drinks in the pub) he 'tagged' along and because it was thought he might be "useful to their career in the future", they let him play guitar with the band. In the past it has always been rumoured that he answered the advert the band put in Melody Maker (Sept 75) and played when the line-up included Johnny Rotten, but that is not true.
Bernie Rhodes, later manager of 'The Clash' was around working with Malcolm McLaren and sometimes gave a little help or offered the band some advice.
Malcolm had ideas about a name for the band and suggested 'The Q.T. Sex Pistols'. Another variation he considered was 'Kutie Jones and his Sex Pistols' and this name even appeared on a T-Shirt that was sold in his shop. Meanwhile, the band were considering calling themselves 'The Strand', after Roxy Music's – Do The Strand. Other names on the list included: 'The Damned', 'Creme de la Creme' and 'Kid Gladlove'.
At first, starting the band had been considered just a laugh, but over this period of time they began to take it more seriously.
Malcolm McLaren and Vivien Westwood change the name of their shop to "SEX".

Would You Buy A Rubber T-Shirt From This Man?

Malcolm McLaren runs a shop called *Sex*. Guess what he has hanging from the wallbars . . .

SLOUCHING DOWN towards the sleazy part of London's Kings Road (which, true to the manic depressive way that cults come and go, has now become the trendy end) is the shop *Sex*. It's not easy to miss. A dark facade, under the inflatable pink mammary vinyl sign, with a cluster of people invariably outside, trying to peer in to prize open its secrets.

Sex comes to us, hot from its co-owners, Malcolm McLaren and Viv Westwood, who titillated themselves before this by owning *Let It Rock*, a teddy boyish clothes shop, and *Too Fast To Live, Too Young To Die*, a brief, punk mod shop.

"We became fed up with TFTL," Malcolm explained as I perused his wares and customers one afternoon. "And we felt that, though we were suddenly making a lot more money than before, that kind of American Fifties style clothing was beginning to loose its bite through the whole nostalgia boom, so we just closed and abandoned the ship while we decided what to do next.

"We became hooked on the idea of opening a gymnasium there, and selling additional stuff like rubber suits and clothes for the body that you can sweat in. That's the idea of the wallbars."

Sure enough, the rubber T-shirts, skirts and suits, leather jackets, political and sexual torn T-shirts, cock rings, masks and vinyl tops hang mostly on the bars I'd never noticed during my fleeting visits to the shop.

"Then gradually we became more and more excited about producing clothes for the body. Of course, there already existed a market for sensual clothing. But it was too underground, predominantly a mail-order phenomenon — not at all for the young, for the kind of clientele I'd already established."

But though many of the clothes at *Sex* are meant to materialize one's widest sexual fantasies and the sensations arising from them, the shop does want to present a serious rationale for its wares.

"Wearing these clothes will affect your social life," *Sex* promises. "Ordinary fashion is just concerned with beauty factors to the exclusion of social ones."

People thumbing through the "dirty T-shirts" on display do stop and read (its effect has been in some cases to make them write their own words on T-shirts), and at what other shop will you get laughter and giggling coming from behind a screen as an American girl tries on a leather T-shirt with zips on the breasts?

A short while ago the laughter stopped for a while. *Sex* was busted for obscenity — the first time a fashion item has been so prosecuted. The T-shirt had finally taken its revenge on *Lady Chatterley's Lover*.

"A guy was busted for wearing our nude cowboy T-shirt in Picadilly. The T-shirt basically shows two cowboys outside a saloon with their pants down. I designed it as a social joke, and we got prosecuted under the 1824 Vagrancy Act, which is a joke in itself, as it's one of the acts that can't be tried by jury."

Throughout our conversation, Malcolm puts forward the analogy of *Sex* as being like the Teddy Boy shop he had previously, and not only from the angle of affronting the establishment. Until *Let It Rock* appeared he says, Teddy Boys of the Seventies never had a shop where they could peruse clothes; and so, up till now, neither had the sexual fetishist. "Of course, they seem a bit estranged at first with the other clientele and the brighter lights, but they tell me we do harbour some interesting masks.

"The clothes, like Teddy Boy fashion," Malcolm optimistically opines in search of a theory behind the threads, "are an affront to the established way of doing things. Just the idea of a 16-year-old girl from the suburbs turning up in a rubber mini skirt, as a lot of them do, to the office in the morning . . . they become involved and socially, as well as sensually, stimulated; much more so than someone in conventional clothing."

Malcolm predicts that one of the things about his shop is the cult it could start. And, forever the astute businessman, he already has a club for them to hang out in.

"I think now that kids have a hankering to be part of a movement (like the Teddy Boys of the Fifties and the Mods of the Sixties). They want to be

"I've always been involved with cults — the subterranean influence on people — that's what fashion is predominantly about. The fashion market at the moment has separated the kids into all different factors. They can be fashionable either by going to the Portobello, or a chain like *Take Six*, or something chic like *Stirling Cooper*, because all commercialism feeds on diversification.

the same, to associate with a movement that's hard and tough and in the open like the clothes we're selling here."

And what of the future? We'll try to make our clothes more seditious and militant and not so unpractical." But how could any shop be more seditious than *Sex*? Any shop that sells its sex wares upfront while it illicitly hides its Rocker Winkle Picker shoes and Drape jackets from view at the back, is already seditious.

Rick Szymanski

FRIDAY, AUGUST, 8, 1975

'Indecent' display in King's Road shop alleged

CHELSEA shop - owners Malcolm McLaren (29) and Miss Vivien Westwood (34), both of Thurleigh Court, Nightingale Road, Balham, were at Marlborough Street last week remanded on bail until August 18th, accused of exposing to public view an indecent exhibition on a display rack at the shop, Sex, in King's Road, Chelsea.

Remanded to another court

CHELSEA shop-owners Malcolm McLaren (29), Miss Vivien Westwood (both of Thurlington Co Nightingale Road, Balha were again remanded on when they appeared Marlborough Street Court cently accused of exposing public view an indecent exhi tion at the shop Sex in Kin Road.

The couple were remanded the Wells Street Court whe their case comes up again November 27th.

EARLY 1975

The line-up of Steve, Paul, Glen and Wally give their one and only public performance when they get up and play 3 songs at a party held in a flat above Tom Salters Cafe, 205 Kings Road in Chelsea. The songs were probably 'Roadrunner'/'Whatcha Gonna Do About It' and 'Scarface'. If they were using a name at this time (which is unlikely) it was "The Strand" and not "The Swankers" as most people seem to think.

SPRING 1975

After nearly 6 months of working with "The New York Dolls", at the end of which they split-up, Malcolm McLaren returned from the USA. He brought back a White Gibson Les Paul guitar that had belonged to either Johnny Thunders or Sylvain Sylvain and this is the guitar that Steve Jones later used on stage.
Malcolm now turned his full attention to Glen, Paul, Steve and Wally's band. He had been acting as their adviser/manager since late 73/early 74 but up until this time without any 'real' commitment. With this renewed enthusiasm it became obvious to Malcolm that Wally didn't really 'look right' or fit in with the others in a way that would allow him to fulfil his idea of a 70's rock band. He decided that a new member would have to be found. So one day when Wally turned up for a rehearsal he was told by Steve Jones that the band wanted him to leave. Steve had already been practising to play the guitar at home and Malcolm suggested that he should change to the position of guitarist, and so the hunt was on for a new frontman. Wally however, feels that Steve realising that he didn't have what it takes to be a vocalist, decided to swop to guitar and 'pushed' Malcolm into this decision.

JUNE/JULY 1975

Malcolm's choice for a vocalist was Richard Hell who sported a short spiky haircut and ripped clothes. Until late 74/early 75 he'd been a member of New York band "Television". He had since formed "The Heartbreakers" with Johnny Thunders. However the band wanted someone unknown and from the London area. Malcolm continued to talk of people like Johnny Thunders and Sylvain Sylvain and he got Glen to speak to Midge Ure (then in a band called "Slik") but the band always thought of this as "just small talk" and continued to look for someone they wanted.

AUGUST 1975

One Saturday afternoon sometime in August (possibly 23rd), John Lydon walked in to Malcolm's shop. He had recently become a regular customer and the band had noticed him on one of his previous visits because of his green hair and they "kinda liked his attitude"! After a short chat they arranged a meeting at a nearby pub called The Roebuck (354 Kings Road). His audition was to sing along to Alice Cooper's record 'School's Out' (Paul Cook says it was 'Eighteen'!) in front of the juke box at Malcolm's shop. He passed!
This was the birth of the "Sex Pistols", the name having been decided upon by Malcolm some time before.

Page 66—MELODY MAKER, September 13, 1975

Property

15p per word

TIN PAN ALLEY. Must be useful for some msicians, agents or such. To take over. Small lock-up premises. Store gear, group-meet, rehearse, hire-it-out, etc. Sacrifice. — 455 7487.

MELODY MAKER, September 27, 1975

Page 56 *Musicians Wanted*

WHIZZ KID GUITARIST

Not older than 20

Not worse looking than Johnny Thunders

Auditioning:

TIN PAN ALLEY

Ring 351 0764, 673 0855

I did you no wrong (words)

Understanding

Scarface (words & music)

We're Pretty Vacant (music)

I'm on a Submarine mission for your love (music)

you're driving me wild (music

lazy ~~[illegible]~~ sod (lyrics)

Gamble & Procter

Substitute

All or nothing (slow)

(shake appeel)

I've got a feeling

Two little sisters ~~[illegible]~~

found strangled in their bedroom

All alone

Johnny's idea for song lyrics which were never used.

The band began rehearsing at a place called the Crunchie Frog in Rotherhithe. This was where Johnny had agreed to sing with the band for the first time after his 'audition'. However, all but Johnny failed to turn up for this first meeting and it took some persuading before he would attend a further rehearsal. Only two or three practices took place here before they moved to a rehearsal room above a pub in Wandsworth called the Rose & Crown. It cost the band £8 per session but was not properly soundproofed, so they only used it for about a week. It was here that John Grey, a friend of Johnny's, took some snapshots of the band. These are almost certainly the very earliest photos taken of the Sex Pistols. About three rehearsals then took place behind the Roundhouse in Chalk Farm. On one of these occasions an Orchestra were playing there. The band were asked to 'turn down the volume of their equipment' because the Orchestra were being recorded for a radio broadcast. However, these requests were ignored and so 'somewhere' there is a recording of an Orchestra accompanied by the Sex Pistols rehearsing!

SEPTEMBER 1975

In Melody Maker (Sept 13), a small advert appeared in the classifieds offering a small room to let at 6 Denmark Street just off Charing Cross Road. Malcolm asked Glen Matlock to phone up and a deal was struck. This became the band's rehearsal studio and a place for Steve to live. Paul was reluctant to give up his day job as an electrician's mate, working for a brewery, and said he thought Steve was pretty awful as a guitarist and was threatening to leave. So Malcolm placed a small advert in the 'Musicians Wanted' section of Melody Maker for a "Whizz Kid Guitarist" to increase the band to a five.piece. The advert appeared in the issue dated the 27th of September. Among the many who answered the advert was Steve New, then only 15 years old. He auditioned and stayed for a couple of rehearsals, but the band soon decided that Steve Jones was improving and they didn't really need another member.

OCTOBER 1975

The line-up was now: Paul Cook - Drums, Steve Jones - Guitar and backing vocals, Glen Matlock - Bass Guitar and backing vocals and John Rotten - on Vocals (only later 'Johnny' with his new surname invented by Steve Jones because he was always saying "You're Rotten, You Are"). Since Johnny joined they had been rehearsing songs such as 'Psychotic Reaction' - Count Five, 'A Day Without Love' - Love Affair, 'All Or Nothing', 'My Mind's Eye', 'Hey Girl', 'Understanding' & 'Sha La La La Lee' (which the band often referred to as 'Gamble & Proctor') all by the Small Faces, 'Holy Cow' - Lee Dorsey, 'Roadrunner' (the Jonathan Richman song), 'Slow Death' - Flamin' Groovies, 'I'm Not Like Everybody Else' - The Kinks, 'Substitute' and 'I'm A Boy' - The Who, 'No Lip' - Dave Berry plus 'Shake', 'Watch Your Step' and a song introduced by Johnny called 'Thru My Eyes' - The Creation. They also included some self penned songs; 'Younger Generation' (at one time called 'Mindless Generation'), 'Raising Rabbits' (early version of 'Lonely Boy'), 'I Did You No Wrong', 'Submission', 'Go Now' (written by Glen), 'Seventeen', 'We're Pretty Vacant', 'Kill Me Today', 'Old Fashioned' (also known by another title?), 'Concrete Youth', and 'I'm Happy'.

W.C.

WESTFIELD COLLEGE NEWSPAPER

FREE

vol. 1   no. 3

MOBIUS CONCERT STORM

Last Friday, 21st November, saw an amazing reaction by students at Westfield to the College Administration's restrictions on the use of the main refectory as a concert hall.

Some years ago the students of the time agreed (under protest) to a system of rationing of the main refectory for major Ents events. This allowed them three bookings in the first term, two in the second and one in the final term (though these figures did not include the Christmas and Summer Balls, which are also attended by staff). Ever since this agreement came into being the Union at Westfield, and its members, have felt it to be an unnecessary and unfair restriction on the social life of the student body, and have been pressing for a more realistic attitude from the Principal and his staff.

Last year resentment grew dramatically after a number of requests from record companies to record live albums at Westfield had to be declined as it was not possible to obtain use of the refectory because the quota of booking for the term had been used.

At a UGM held on the 6th of November this term a motion was passed which clarified Union policy on the matter. It instructed the Executive to initiate negotiation with College to allow twenty events each year in the refectory, and to improve upon the finishing times currently imposed (although the Union is financially incapable of putting on this number of main events, it would mean that groups such as the Arts Workshop or Pheonix could put on plays etc.).

Then it was learned that Mobius wished to perform at Westfield for just the cost of their expences (the directors of Island Records

were planning to watch then at a concert, and Mobius are particularly fond of Westfield College). A meeting organised by Ents societies was held at which it was decided to go ahead and stage the concert on the 21st, even though the terms quota had already been exceeded by holding the Barn Dance.

While advance tickets were being sold Mr. Parkin, College Secretary, was informed as to how the situation stood. He promptly gave his permission, much to the dissappointment of some more athletic members of the Union.

At four o'clock on the afternoon of the concert a second group, the Sex Pistols, telephoned the Union office to say that they were willing to play for free. At seven o'clock in the evening a third group, Factory, indicated that they would also play at the concert for free. Andy Stewart found himself in the enviable position of having organised a three group concert, with a disco, charging only 10p door and having made a profit, though it had been budgeted to loose about £10 – 20.

When later that evening, during the last group's performance, the gentlemen of Security, acting under College instructions, turned on the lights in the refectory, the audience demonstrated their displeasure by gaining entrance to the dining hall servery, where the light switches are located, removing the Security man, and turning the lights back off.

Mike Lilly, the Senior Tutor, was summoned, and it was agreed that the entrance to the servery could be locked, with Security and students outside and with the lights off, until the end of the concert, the time of which could be decided by the audience. When the last group had finished the disco came on, and at 12:30 Andy Stewart, having talked with Dr. Lilly, suggested an end. He was immediately and vociferously overrulled from the floor, and the disco continued for about half an hour.

It is to be hoped that College, who have admitted that it is time for the matter to be reviewed, take heed of this demonstration of the will of the Westfield student body, and speed up their administrative machine, so that no further confrontations need take place.

What is it that this man has seen? Turn to page 5 for the answer. Photo Paul Johnston.

6 THUR   The Sex Pistols play their first ever live concert in a little
          upstairs room at St. Martin's School of Art, 107 Charing Cross
Road, London WC2. They play 5 songs before someone cuts the power
supply. The main band are called "Bazooka Joe", a Rock'n'Roll revival
band that boasts Stuart Goddard as a member. This young man later
changed his name to "Adam Ant". Adam recalls the songs the Sex Pistols
played that night included: 'No Lip', 'Substitute', 'Seventeen' and
'Whatcha Gonna Do About It'. The Sex Pistols had to carry their own
equipment all the way from the rehearsal room in Denmark Street because
the main band refused to let them borrow any!

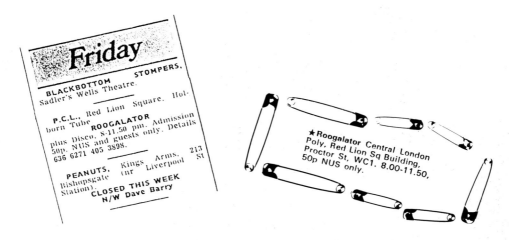

7 FRI   Sex Pistols play Central School of Art & Design in Holborn.
          This building is connected to the Facility of Law department
of the Polytechnic of Central London and they play in the PCL's 1st floor
Cafeteria on a specially built stage. This gig is as support to a band
called "Roogalator". They play their complete set which lasts for about 30
minutes. The admission price is 50p but open to NUS members and their
guests only. For their first 3 or 4 gigs Glen Matlock sings lead vocal on
a song he has written called 'Go Now' (not the Moody Blues song). John
hates it! This gig became possible because the social secretary, Sebastian
Conran (son of Terence Conran, the Habitat tycoon) and his friend Al
McDowell saw the band the previous night and loved them. They also
think any band called the Sex Pistols must be alright!

21 FRI   The Sex Pistols play Westfield College at Frognal, Finchley
          Road, London, NW3. The concert is almost cancelled after the
student union overspend their term budget, however the Sex Pistols phone
the college and tell them they are willing to play for nothing! The main
band are a 'hippy band' called Mobias and 3rd on the bill are a band
called Factory.

28 FRI   Sex Pistols play at the Xmas Ball of Queen Elizabeth College,
          (now Kensington site) Campden Hill Road, Kensington, W8.
There are five other bands playing in various rooms. Georgie Fame & the
Blue Flames are top of the bill and play in a different room. All the
students are dressed in formal attire, black suits with dickie bow ties.

The earliest known live photos in existence, taken at Chelsea, December 5 1975.

<u>5 FRI</u>   Sex Pistols play Chelsea School of Art, Manresa Road, SW3. In these very early days Malcolm always preferred a disco to a live support band because he feels that all other bands are so "out of step" with the Sex Pistols music. No other live band played on this occasion.

<u>9 TUE</u>   Sex Pistols play Ravensbourne College of Art in Chislehurst close to Bromley, as support to a band called Fogg who travel all the way down from Newcastle upon Tyne. To begin with the hall is fairly crowded but the Sex Pistols music is not to the taste of the audience and the hall soon clears as people make for the bar. However, they are seen by Simon Barker who tells some of his friends. These people later make up what has become known as 'The Bromley Contingent'. The other members of the Contingent (at one time or another) include: Suzie (later Siouxsie), Steven Bailey (later Havoc later Severin), William Broad (later known as Billy Idol), Sue (Lucas) Catwoman, Debbie (Wilson) Juvenile, Tracie O'Keefe and Berlin. Songs the Sex Pistols perform include 'Thru My Eyes'.

EVENTS WHERE EXACT DATE IS UNKNOWN:

Sex Pistols play North East London Polytechnic?

Sex Pistols play St. Albans, Hertfordshire College of Art & Design.

Sex Pistols play City of London Poly, opposite Aldgate East Tube Station?

Between November and the end of February the Sex Pistols gatecrash various colleges around the outskirts of London by posing as the official support band. A handful of other dates are thought to exist but no further information is known at present.

Sex Pistols play as support to Dave Berry (60's pop star) – details unknown – Paul Cook says no?

Sex Pistols play as support to City Boy – details unknown – Paul Cook thinks this is probably the gig with Mr Big at Welwyn (Feb 21st)?

Sex Pistols play North East London Poly?

Sex Pistols play in the upstairs room of a pub in London's East Ham/West Ham or Aldgate area. Bernie Rhodes drives the equipment van, they arrive late! They are stopped halfway through their set – date and further details unknown.

Susan Janet Ballion (Siouxsie) and Steve Bailey (later Havoc later Severin) witness the Sex Pistols for the first time (location unknown).

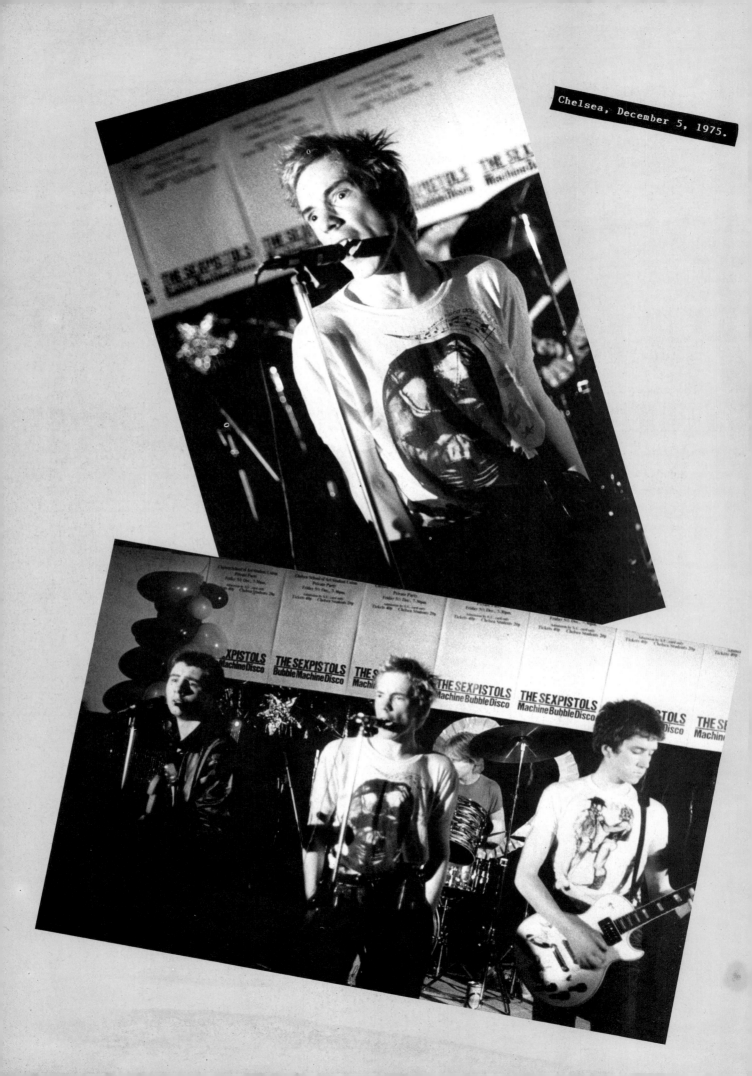

Don't look over your shoulder, but the Sex Pistols are coming

Sex Pistols
MARQUEE

"HURRY UP, they're having an orgy on stage," said the bloke on the door as he tore the tickets up.

I waded to the front and staightway sighted a chair arcing gracefully through the air, skidding across the stage and thudding contentedly into the PA system, to the obvious nonchalance of the bass drums and guitar.

Well I didn't think they sounded *that* bad on first earful — then I saw it was the singer wh'd done the throwing.

He was stalking round the front rows, apparently scuffing over the litter on the floor between baring his teeth at the audience and stopping to chat to members of the group's retinue. He's called Johnny Rotten and the moniker fits.

Sex Pistols? Seems I'd missed the cavortings with the two scantily clad (plastic thigh boots

and bodices) pieces dancing up front. In fact, I only caught the last few numbers; enough, as it happens, to get the idea. Which is . . a quarter of spiky teenage misfits from the wrong end of various London roads, playing 60's styled white punk rock as unself-consciously as it's possible to play it these days i.e. self consciously.

Punks' Springsteen Bruce and the rest of 'em would get shredded if they went up against these boys. They've played less than a dozen gigs as yet, have a small but fanatic following, and don't get asked back. Next month they play the Institute of Contemporary Arts if that's a clue.

I'm told the Pistols repertoire includes lesser known Dave Berry and Small Faces numbers (check out early Kinks' B sides leads), besides an Iggy and the Stooges item and several self penned numbers like the moronic "I'm Pretty Vacant," a meandering power-chord job that produced the chair throwing incident

No-one asked for an encore but they did one anyway.

"We're going to play 'Substitute'."

"You can't play," heckled an irate French punter.

"So what?" countered the bassman, jutting his chin in the direction of the bewildered Frog.

That's how it is with the Pistols — a musical experience with the emphasis on Experience.

"Actually, we're not into music," one of the Pistols confided afterwards.

Wot then?

"We're into chaos."

Neil Spencer

2 MON   Aylesbury? – Live recordings of this date are fakes, taken from the Nashville Rooms (April '76) with the order of songs changed round. Indeed, aside from these fake recordings there is no evidence to suggest they even played in Aylesbury.

12 THUR   Sex Pistols support Eddie & the Hot Rods at the Marquee club in London and damage some of the Hot Rods equipment, probably due to the chairs that Johnny throws around. They make a quick exit. Their set includes the use of Jordan appearing semi-nude. Songs played include 'Pretty Vacant' and an un-asked for encore of 'Substitute'. This gig was obtained by Glen and Johnny after they had approached the manager of the club and simply asked if their band could play!

14 SAT   Sex Pistols perform at a party held by Andrew Logan (famous Artist/Sculptor/London Socialite) at his spacious studio cum warehouse at Butler's Wharf, Tower Bridge, situated close to the River Thames. Jordan appears onstage and strips naked to the waist. Chrissie Hynde (later in the Pretenders) and most of the 'Bromley Contingent' are here. Derek Jarman films the band on a hand held Super 8 camera and you can see a small part of this in "The Great Rock'n'Roll Swindle". The 'stage' consists of the set from the court scene in the film 'Sebastion' together with a Castle that Andrew Logan purchased from the children's department of Biba's store in Kensington that recently closed.

19 THUR   St. Albans, Hertfordshire College of Art & Design. Songs performed: 'Did You No Wrong'/'No Lip'/'Understanding'/'New York'/'Seventeen'/'Steppin' Stone'/'Submission'/'No Fun'/'Whatcha Gonna Do About It'/'Pretty Vacant'/'Substitute' (**).

Pete Shelley and Howard Devoto (who later formed the Buzzcocks) read a review in New Musical Express of the Sex Pistols appearance at the Marquee club, including the fact that they play a song by Iggy & the Stooges. With the offer from a friend (Richard Boon, later manager of the Buzzcocks) of spending a few days in Reading (40 miles from London), they decide to see the Sex Pistols play live. Time Out (London's 'what's on' guide) gives no details of where they might be playing, so they phone NME and speak to someone who informs them that the Sex Pistols manager runs a shop called "Sex" at 430 Kings Road, Chelsea. Pete and Howard visit the address and speak with Malcolm McLaren who informs them of the gigs on the 20th and 21st. They travel to both!

20 FRI   The Sex Pistols are one of the three bands at Bucks College of Higher Education Valentine's Dance in High Wycombe. The main band (who they borrow equipment from) is Screaming Lord Sutch. Some equipment including a rare vintage microphone gets damaged, allegedly by Johnny Rotten.

21 SAT   Welwyn Garden City as support to Mr Big. Songs performed 'Did You No Wrong'/'No Lip'/'Understanding'/'New York'/'Seventeen'/'Whatcha Gonna Do About It'/'Submission'/'Steppin' Stone'/'Pretty Vacant'/'No Fun'/'Substitute' (**).

The symbol (**) indicates a live bootleg recording exists

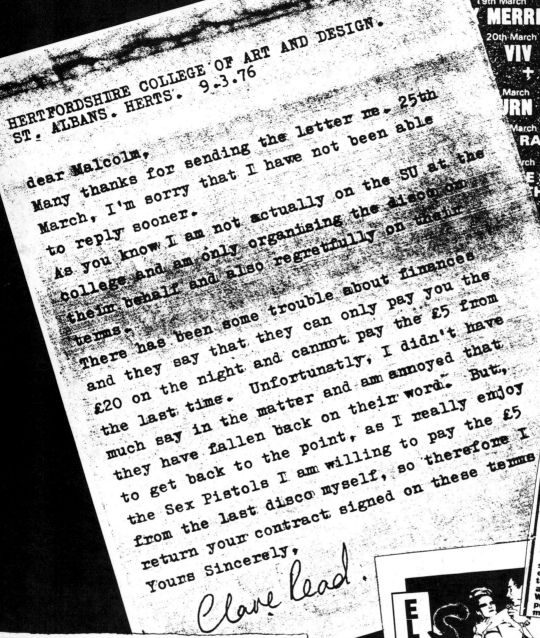

HERTFORDSHIRE COLLEGE OF ART AND DESIGN.
ST. ALBANS. HERTS. 9.3.76

dear Malcolm,

Many thanks for sending the letter re. 25th
March, I'm sorry that I have not been able
to reply sooner.
As you know I am not actually on the SU at the
college and am only organising the disco on
their behalf and also regretfully on their
terms.
There has been some trouble about finances
and they say that they can only pay you the
£20 on the night and cannot pay the £5 from
the last time. Unfortunatly, I didn't have
much say in the matter and am annoyed that
they have fallen back on their word. But,
to get back to the point, as I really enjoy
the Sex Pistols I am willing to pay the £5
from the last disco myself, so therefore I
return your contract signed on these terms

Youns Sincerely,

Clave lead.

16 TUES Notices in various gig guides mention that the Sex Pistols are to play the Nashville in West Kensington, London as support to the Stranglers but this is a mistake.

20 SAT Adverts in the music papers state the Sex Pistols will appear at the Nashville as support to Viv Stanshall but this is not true.

23 TUES The music paper gig guides once again state the band will be supporting the Stranglers at the Nashville on this date but again this is incorrect.

25 THUR The Sex Pistols play St. Albans, Hertfordshire College of Art & Design. They are paid £20. There are no other live acts, just a disco.

30 TUES Sex Pistols play the 100 club in London's Oxford Street for the very first time. Booked by promoter Ron Watts after he saw them at High Wycombe in February (20th). This is the night that Johnny tries to pick a fight with Glen Matlock while still on stage and one of a few times when the band nearly split up in 1976. Other bands playing are "Plummet Airlines" (headlining act) and "Salt" (bottom of the bill). Adverts bill the show as 'New Band Night'. About 50 people turn up and probably about 30 of these came to see the other bands!

3 SAT The Nashville Rooms, 171 North End Road West Kensington in London as support to Joe Strummer's band, the 101'ers. Songs performed by the Sex Pistols: 'Did You No Wrong'/'No Lip'/'Seventeen'/ 'Steppin' Stone'/'No Feelings'/'New York'/'No Fun'/'Submission'/'Substitute'/'Problems'/'Satellite'/'Pretty Vacant' plus encore 'Understanding'/ 'Did You No Wrong' (**). This is the gig where Dave Goodman first works as the band's sound engineer and starts to create a 'wall of sound' that includes adding echo to Johnny's vocal and certainly helps to 'mould' their unique sound. Admission price is 50p. The Sex Pistols are paid £25 of which they have to pay £20 for the hire of a sound system.

4 SUN Malcolm McLaren and the Sex Pistols promote their own gig at the El Paradise strip club in Brewer Street, Soho in London. Johnny wears 'granny glasses' for part of the set. Songs played include 'Stepping Stone'. Printed handbills are given out to advertise the event. Jonh Ingham of Sounds witnesses the band for the first time.

10 SAT Melody Maker includes a review of the Sex Pistols live and comments "They do as much for music as World War Two did for the cause of peace and I hope we shall hear no more of them". The review is from their gig at the Nashville a week earlier.

17 SAT   New Musical Express includes a review of the Nashville gig.

18 SUN   A second proposed gig at the El Paradise strip club in
            London's Soho is planned for this date but it never takes
            place.

23 FRI   The Nashville Rooms as support to the 101'ers. Entrance price
            is £1.00. Ted Carroll is DJ and famous for playing records by
the Small Faces, the Creation, Iggy & the Stooges, the New York Dolls
and generally a style that suits the Sex Pistols. Songs performed: 'Did
You No Wrong'/'No Lip'/'Seventeen'/'New York'/'Whatcha Gonna Do About
It'/'Steppin' Stone'/'Submission'/'Satellite'/'No Feelings'/'Pretty Vacant'/
'No Fun'/'Substitute'/'Problems' (**). This is the night of the infamous
fight when as rumour has it, Vivien Westwood picks on a member of the
audience and 3 of the band then join in. The band are banned after this
event but manage to play here the following week by hiring the venue
under the pretext of using it for a 'private party' (29th).

24 SAT   The first full length article on the band appears in 'Sounds'.
            Two pages written by Jonh Ingham.

29 THUR   The Nashville Rooms in London, this time as the headline
            band. To help promote the gig printed handbills are given out
that say 'Party with the Sex Pistols'. Support is Ted Carroll's Rock On
disco. The admission price is 50p.

SEX PISTOLS
Are at the 100 CLUB

Tuesday May 18th, 25th at 8 pm

AND AT THE SCREEN ON THE GREEN (ISLINGTON) At Midnight on
Monday May 17th

100 CLUB
TUESDAY'S IN MAY
11, 18 & 25
100 OXFORD ST.

THE SEX PISTOL MANAGEMENT
wishes to apologise for any inconvenience caused as a result of the sudden cancellation of The Screen on Islington Green venue on Monday 17th May midnight

SEX PISTOLS "secretly" recording with Chris Spedding recently; an enthused Spedding producing three of their own numbers (I'm Pretty Vacant", "No Feelings", "Problems") and we bet it makes him feel his age (vide famous refusal by John Rotten of Star Rock Journalist's request to jam with the band: "You're too old and you're hair's too long") . . .

SEX PISTOLS
Sole representation and management:
Malcolm McLaren
93 Bell Street, London, N.W.1.
01-673 0855   01-723 7982

RECEIVED 1 8 MAY 1976

Alan Morrison,
~~3rd Floor,~~
Zetland House,
Zetland Road,
Middlesborough.

re - The Sex Pistols.
Confirmation and contract.

An agreement made the 11th May
by telephone. Between. Malcolm McLaren (manager Sex Pistols)
1976. and Alan Morrison (Promotion).

to play at The Middlesborough
Town Hall Albert Road. Middlesborough on
Friday 21st May 1976 The fee discussed of £20 to
be paid in cash, on the night, to the band.
The group's arrival time will
be 3pm. To commence performance at
8pm Playing time 1½ hours approx,
Please accept this letter as
confirmation and contract. and sign where
~~appropriate.~~ and return letter signed as soon
as possible. Thank-you,

signed. M McLaren

Promoter's Signature. Alan Morris. P.P. Middlesborough Council

DOCTORS OF MADNESS

 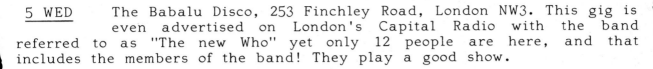

MAY 1976

5 WED   The Babalu Disco, 253 Finchley Road, London NW3. This gig is even advertised on London's Capital Radio with the band referred to as "The new Who" yet only 12 people are here, and that includes the members of the band! They play a good show.

6 THUR   North East London Poly?

11 TUES   The 100 club in London's Oxford Street with support band Krakotoa.

17 MON   The Screen on the Green, Islington, London – cancelled.

18 TUE   The 100 club in London plus support band Strange Days.

19 WED   Northallerton in North Yorkshire where they are introduced with the words: "and now ladies and gentlemen, for the very first time up north, in cabaret, the Sex Pistols".

20 THUR   Scarborough, Penthouse.

21 FRI   Middlesborough Town Hall, The Crypt – as support to the Doctors of Madness. The contract states that they should play for 1 hour 30 minutes but whether they do or not is unknown. Their 'usual set' at this time lasts for less than 1 hour. They are paid £20.

25 TUES   The 100 club, plus support band Dogwatch. Ted Carroll's Rock On disco spins the records (Ted also runs Chiswick records).

30 SUN   Reading University, Art Department.

EVENTS WHERE EXACT DATE IS UNKNOWN:

They may also have played in Whitby and at a teachers training college in York or Lincoln during May?

It was at the regular Tuesday night gigs of the Sex Pistols playing the 100 club at this time that Sid Vicious invents the Pogo dance!

Sex Pistols spend one day in Majestic Studios, London SW4 with producer Chris Spedding and record 3 songs: 'Problems'/'No Feelings'/'Pretty Vacant'. In 1981 all 3 songs appeared on a German 7" bootleg EP.

Malcolm McLaren calls on promoter John Curd to ask him if the Sex Pistols can support the Ramones at their forthcoming Roundhouse gig. They speak to Curd's wife who tells Malcolm that he has seen the band and doesn't like them. Malcolm and his assistant Nils Stevenson (who later becomes the manager of Siouxsie & The Banshees) tell Curd's wife that the man must be an arsehole not to book the band. John Curd (who has been in the next room eating his lunch) appears and a fight ensues. Malcolm gets thrown down the stairs.

Members of the Sex Pistols attend a party held by Berlin, one of the Bromley contingent. Parts of the party are filmed on super 8.

Sex Pistols

So there we were. Priding ourselves on attractive elitism upwards of seventy or so cross sectioned furry freaks and plastic poseurs politely settled in the quaintly draped hitherto mysterious Lesser Free Trade Hall. There to see a youthful contemporary quartet play the street avant garde music of the sixties in its properly repressed seventies setting. The Sex Pistols. Plenty of ripe s's in the name, the surging s rock very much inbred into the Pistols controlled chaotic punk muzak. Acceptably stylised, thankfully few traces of commonplace modern ill posturing, the sound owes not a little to two of the few genuine geniuses in rock, Iggy Pop and Ray Davies. Visually, without the purposeful, powerful musical support, they falter. Mild manneredsfresh faced youths, perhaps uncouth, on leave from their self-imposed army sentence. Johnny Rotten, lead singer, possesses a cute carrot coloured overgrown crew cut and commences the set with ansice pair of small oblong stamp-sized shades that place him at about grade two menace-punk. When he whips them off, he shrinks alarmingly, we see the whites of his beady eyes and he's a grade two weed. No matter. The rough, raw tidal surge transforms the quartet into one neat unit of aloof intimidating punks. Guitar, bass, adopt suitable respectable easy-split stances. Rotten plays Frankenstein playing Lionel Blair with a hint of the forced mechanism of Bowie, Ferry and Bygraves. Technically they're accomplished. Defined limits, but they're disciplined and don't stray. Hard, loud, clean, brisk and as relentless and as guiltless as a zipless fuck. Their harmonies are spot off. If one of their songs ventures past the 200 second mark, they contentedly sustain the nifty moronic monotonous peak they initially attained. They plagiarise admirably. The Stooges 'No Fun'. The Monkees 'I'm Not Your Stepping Stone', 'Substitute' by the Who (an obscure sixties sub-cult who now do cabaret and dated 'freaky' films). The Pistols' own songs are London mirror takes of verlaines New York violent rejections and sexual rebuttals. They're excellent.

Aggression through repression. Get on with it.

SEX PISTOLS
are at
MANCHESTER LESSER
FREE TRADE HALL
on Friday, June 4th
at 7.30 pm.

<u>4 FRI</u>   Manchester, Lesser Free Trade Hall. Songs performed: 'Did You
         No Wrong'/'No Lip'/'Seventeen'/'Steppin' Stone'/'New York'/
'Whatcha Gonna Do About It'/'Submission'/'Satellite'/'No Feelings'/'No
Fun'/'Substitute'/'Pretty Vacant plus two encores 'Problems'/'No Fun'
(**). Among the 70 people who turn up are Bernard Dicken, Peter Hook
and Ian Curtis, later all members of 'Joy Division' and Stephen Morrissey,
later with 'The Smiths'. Tickets cost 50p.

<u>15 TUES</u>   The 100 club supported by the 101'ers. This is to be the
         101'ers last ever gig. They have already decided to break up
         following tonight's show.

<u>17 THUR</u>   Sex Pistols take over the support slot at the Midsummer Music
         Festival Benefit concert at Walthamstow Assembly Hall, after
the demise of the 101'ers. The main band is Ian Dury & the Kilburns.
The Stranglers also play a few numbers but keep it short because some of
the equipment is faulty and they think they might be electrocuted.
Admission price is 95p.

<u>29 TUES</u>   The 100 club, Oxford Street, London. Support band is Seventh
         Heaven. Songs performed: 'Flowers of Romance'/'Seventeen'/'No
Lip'/'Steppin' Stone'/'New York'/'Whatcha Gonna Do About It'/'Submis-
sion'/'I Wanna Be Me'/'Satellite'/'No Feelings'/'No Fun'/'Substitute'/
'Problems'/'Pretty Vacant' and an encore of 'Did You No Wrong' (**).
This is almost certainly the first time they ever play 'Flowers of
Romance' in public. A superb performance that captures the 'rapport'
Johnny is building up with the audience by playing at the 100 club on a
regular basis. Towards the end of their set, Malcolm buys Johnny a
drink (a rare event) and in return receives a dedication as they play
'Substitute'. On the live tapes that exist, after 'Pretty Vacant' you can
hear a voice that sounds remarkably like Malcolm's getting members of
the audience to call the band back on stage for an encore. Whoever it is
succeeds!

Pistols get the bullet

LAST NIGHT I went to see the Sex Pistols and Clash (formerly 101'ers) for the first time. I was very, very disappointed. Both bands were crap. It's enough to turn you on to Demis Roussos.

There is currently far too much publicity being given to pub bands by the music press. Clash were just a cacophonous barrage of noise. The bass guitarist had no idea how to play the instrument and even had to get another member of the band to tune it for him. They tried to play early '60's r'n'b and failed dismally. Dr. Feelgood are not one of my favourite bands, but I know that they could have wiped the floor with Clash.

The Sex Pistols despite having the wierdest bunch of followers in the audience, (and what a set of freaks they were) were even worse. John Rotten really lived up to his name. I've heard Mickey Mouse sing better. The rest of the band are average musicians, but all the material they played was the same.

At the end, Rotten stayed on the stage and shouted at the audience. One of his comments summed it all up:— "We were great, and you know it. We must have been; we're from London and any band from London is great."

Pathetic, just pathetic . . .
Yours sincerely — **A real music lover, Sheffield.**

SEX PISTOLS

Tuesday

July 6th

SEX PISTOLS +
100 CLUB   the Damned
100 OXFORD ST W.1.   TUESDAY JULY 6

8 – 12 pm
LATE BAR

100 CLUB

3 SAT   Hastings, Pier Pavilion with heavy metal band 'Budgie'.

New Musical Express runs a review by Phil McNeill of the 100 club on the 29th of June.

The 'Jaws' section of Sounds includes an article quoting a press release from the Sex Pistols management over a fight at the 100 club between Sid Vicious and Nick Kent, Michael Beale (Eddie & the Hot Rods management) and an employee from Island records. It also mentions "In the Sex Pistols wake are such bands as Slaughter & the Dogs, Subway Sex (Sect) and Suburban Bolts (Dogs)".

4 SUN   Sheffield, Black Swan supported by the Clash playing their
           first ever public performance. It's amazing to think that two days later the Damned make their debut and on the 20th of this month the Buzzcocks play their first gig. This really must go down in history as the month that 'punk' started!

6 TUES   First "real" gig of the Damned at the 100 club supporting the
           Sex Pistols. The Damned had previously played 4 consecutive Saturdays at a gay place in Lisson Grove. Songs the Sex Pistols perform: 'I Wanna Be Me'/'No Lip'/'Seventeen'/'Steppin' Stone'/'New York'/'Whatcha Gonna Do About It'/'Submission'/'Satellite'/'No Fun'/ 'Substitute'/'Pretty Vacant'/'Problems' (**).

9 FRI   Sex Pistols play at an all-night concert at the Lyceum,
           London as support to the Pretty Things and Supercharge.

10 SAT   The Sundown in
           London's Charing Cross Road. They play for about 30/40 minutes starting at midnight. They are supposed to play two sets but they are not allowed to play the second time.

13 TUES   First issue of Sniffin'
           Glue fanzine appears edited by Mark P. (The P stands for Perry). This issue includes articles on the Ramones, the Flamin' Groovies, the Stranglers, Blue Oyster Cult, the Runaways, Television, Eddie & the Hot Rods, the 101'ers and Todd Rundgren. It also mentions the Damned.

Rock Garden in London's Covent Garden. They were booked to play here but the gig was cancelled at short notice by the management of the club.

ON THE ROAD

SEX PISTOLS: improving from gig to gig

Anarchy in the UK

Sex Pistols/ Slaughter And The Dogs/Buzzcocks

Manchester

ABOVE Manchester's Free Trade Hall is a little known auditorium, capable of holding some 400, cunningly named the Lesser Hall. Until the Sex Pistols discovered it for a concert last month its functional Fifties atmosphere had been sullied only by the strains of the odd jazz recital.

After that concert, which attracted some 150 rough tuff raving Mancunians, conversation led to contact with the fabulously named Slaughter and the Dogs. With the coordination of Howard Devoto, the Pistols organised another bout, the Dogs supporting. In the meantime Devoto whipped his own band, the Buzzcocks, into shape, making for a triple bill of critical mass potential.

Unfortunately, the PA was more expectation than actuality, the Pistols sounds man having to patch together a mismatched jumble of amps to gain results. Under the circumstances, it's a wonder the sound was as good as it was.

It was the Buzzcock's first gig. Devoto stands and sings a lot like Johnny Rotten, and indeed the band sounds a lot like the Pistols, perhaps because Howard hauled guitarist Pete Shelley down to a London Pistols gig so that the light could be seen and the course charted. Whatever their inspiration, they're promising.

Howard, wearing sneakers, pencil thin levis, t-shirt and baggy blue jacket, is singing love songs, the strangest love songs you've ever heard. They have titles like (and I can't vouch for their accuracy) 'Breakout', 'Yuo're Shit',

'Put 'Em Down', 'I Love You, You Big Dummy'. One song goes *I been smoking in the smoking room. Now I'm in the living room, I want what I came for pretty soon.*

It's the Boston Strangler singing the dance of romance, his face getting redder, eyes popping, kicking and punching the air.

At first they are rhythmic to the point of rigidity. Shelley — who is wearing tight salmon pink levis, sleeveless 'Buzzcocks' t-shirt, shades and short hair — not even bothering with the concept of a middle-eight, let alone a solo. The top half of his red, £18.49 Audition guitar is snapped off; he got excited at rehearsal one day and threw it against the wall.

But soon he begins to open out. By the time they fire up a high rev version of the Troggs' 'I Can't Control Myself' he's pulling out all manner of interesting riffs and changes. Drummer John Maher is solid, maintaining a fast, precise rhythm with plenty of cymbal flicking. Bassist Steve Diggle, who has a fair resemblance to Johnny Ramone, is equally strong.

The climax came with a wild feedback solo, Shelley throwing his axe at the amp. When he went on a little too long, Devoto came out of the wings and pulled the guitar from him. He pulled it back. Devoto grabbed all six strings and yanked ripping them asunder. Shelley propped the now screaming guitar against the speaker and left via the audience. Thus finished the set.

Apart from gigs, the only thing the Buzzcocks need is a hell of a lot more volume.

WHILE equipment was changed the capacity audience posed. The David Bowie lookalikes all had the distinct advantage of looking like their skinny hero, perhaps the benefit of plastic surgery. There was a profusion of Neanderthals in stringy hair and leather, one of whom dug the

Pistols by bellowing "Stooges!" and pounding seats to oblivion.

There was a profusion of homemade Slaughter and the Dogs badges, and one trend setter **sported a high-class homemade** Sex Pistols t-shirt. And then there were the six rows of very straight looking people at the back who sat there very vacant all evening, even those who loathed it.

Depending on who you talk to, Slaughter and the Dogs have been alive between eight months and two years; the new order's ground rules are still being formed and no-one is quite sure what's cool to admit and what isn't. Their age is 15 and 16, except for vocalist Wayne Barratt, who sheepishly admits to an ancient 19. Their *raison d'etre*, he says, is to take the energy of 60s Stones to the 70s. An admirable notion, but what this means is that all the fast songs sound like 'Jumping Jack Flash' and the slow ones like 'Angie'.

Anyway you slice it, it is rapidly apparent that the Dogs are well outside the boundaries being drawn by the Pistols. They open with a meandering bass/guitar interchange, the band suddenly bursting on in a blaze of light and noise. For the first tune they generate reasonable excitement, kind of like a high energy Faces routine.

Barratt, who sports immaculately combed green tinted hair, is wearing Captain Blood style brown satin trousers tied at the cuffs, which brush red Anello and Davide shoes. The belt turns into a sash across his chest which somehow turns into a scarf. A codpiece is equipped at no extra charge. The others — Brian Granford (drums), Howard Bates (bass), Mike Day (lead guitar) — look pretty normal, but rhythm guitarist Mike Rossi, who's so punky he can hardly be bothered to mumble his name, is decked out red and white striped t-shirt, black vinyl vest and white Strat; it's a wonder he hasn't dyed his

Ronno hair cut that just so Mick Ronson shade. Ah yes, Slaughter on Tenth Avenue. And naturally, Diamond Dogs.

Just how the Dogs see themselves as being like the Pistols, which is how they approached the group, is an entertaining mystery. It is said that on a local radio show they defined 'punk' as being a cross between David Bowie and the Rolling Stones. But fuck definitions. Pete Shelley reckons they're an offence just to the word itself.

It is also said that a lot of interest is being expressed in them, which is easy to see. They could quite easily replace any of the current crop of 'Top Of The Pops' groups with no drop in visual quality.

They should also learn to differentiate between genuine demand for an encore and a huge scream of relief at their exit. It would save their outnumbered fans a lot of bother.

THE NOTORIOUS Sex Pistols, the band the promoters of the French Punk Rock festival claim are going too far — "Who do they think they are? The Rolling Stones?" — were greeted with a wild ovation. John stood there and beamed. Then Steve jumped to the front of the stage and started ripping off the opening to 'I Want To Be You', legs apart, swinging his hips from side to side. He has great style.

After 'Pushing And Shoving' John takes off his red mohair sweater, the right sleeve of his shirt casually rolled up to show the cigarette burns on his forearm.

At the Lyceum, like a nonchalant robot he'd stuck out his right fist, ground his fag out on it and chucked the butt over his shoulder, all in one fluid, mechanical motion.

The best thing about the Pistols is the rapid improvement they make from gig to gig. Finally hearing John's lyrics gives it quite

a push, but Steve and Glen are really beginning to rein in the power, both piling on the energy through the solos. Unfortunately, Paul's drumming was practically inaudible, but some of the bass runs were real eye-openers, while Steve was rewriting the whole Guitar Hero's Stances textbook, pulling his axe up alongside his cheek (great expression of exquisite pain), firing off early Pete Townshend dive bombs, rocking out on the beat with precise, soaring feedback endings.

It's all summed up in 'I'm A Lazy Sod': *Lotta noise, It's my choice, What I want to do.*

Pretty soon a guy was doing the Wilko Johnson Robot Zigzag at high speed up and down the aisle. People near the front began to jump about more. As the band blasted into 'New York' a guy came leaping down the aisle, each bound taking him about five feet into the air, his feet somewhere around his ears.

'Anarchy In The UK', a new song, was a highpoint: *Give me the MPLA. Or is it UDA. Or is IRA. Or is it the UK. Or just another country. Or just a council tenancy.* 'Satellite', another hot number, has yet to have the lyrics dug out of it, the only visible hook being the chorus, *I love you.* But honey, this ain't no romance, as John disdainfully clarifies. "It's a comment on suburbia, a wife, 2.4 children, a mortgage and a car in the garage."

The closest John Rotten gets to love is the soon-to-be-classic 'No Feelings': *You better understand I'm in love with myself.*

At John's encouragement the front rapidly filled with wildly hopping people. One enthusiastic couple pushed each other back and forth in time to the express train rhythm, and God help anyone in the way. By the time 'Problems' had blasted to a close the joint was screaming.

For an encore, John tore up his shirt. — **JOHN INGHAM.**

Between 13th & 30th   The Sex Pistols record and mix seven high quality demo tracks with Dave Goodman. The backing tracks are laid down at the band's own rehearsal studio in Denmark Street on Dave Goodman's 4 track tape recorder. They are transferred to 8 track plus guitar overdubs and vocals added at Riverside studio, Chiswick, West London. The tracks are then mixed at Decibel studios in North London. The songs are: 'Submission'/'Seventeen'/'Satellite'/'Pretty Vacant'/'Anarchy In The UK'/'No Feelings'/'I Wanna Be Me'
Six of these recordings are issued on 'The Mini Album' on Chaos Records in January 1985. The seventh track was issued on the limited edition picture disc version of 'The Mini Album' in January 1986. A 7" single of 'Submission'/'No Feelings' is issued in a limited issue of 4175 copies, half in yellow vinyl and half in pink vinyl. No black vinyl copies are made. A 12" of 'Submission'/'Anarchy In The UK' is issued in 7 different colours of vinyl, pink being the rarest as only 500 of these are made. Around 12,000 of the 12" are pressed. Early copies of the 12" (excluding pink vinyl) have labels with the catalogue number CARTEL 1 while later copies have EXPORT 1. The version of 'No Feelings' is the one used on the B side of the withdrawn A&M single 'God Save The Queen'.

17 SAT   Dingwalls, London. Rumoured to have played here but they never did. They are banned from here after a rumpus on the 5th in which one or more band members were involved.

20 TUES   Manchester, Lesser Free Trade Hall with support Slaughter & the Dogs and the Buzzcocks. This is the Buzzcocks first gig. This date also marks the very first time that the Sex Pistols play 'Anarchy In The UK' in public.

24 SAT   The National Open Air Music Festival at Burstow Lodge Hill Farm near Gatwick, West Sussex – but the event is cancelled the week before it is due to take place.

Sex Pistols banned

THE SEX PISTOLS have run into trouble with promoters and club owners. They have been pulled out of the French European Punk Rock Festival on August 21 at Mont de Morsan by the promoters who think they have gone 'too far'.

They have also been banned from appearing at London's Dingwalls after the management alleged they were responsible for an incident during the recent Flaming Groovies and Ramones concert when a door was broken and a bottle thrown at Joey Ramone on stage.

They have also been banned from London's Rock Garden.

7 SAT   Sex Pistols appear on the front cover of Melody Maker plus inside is a two page article "Punk Rock: crucial or phoney?".

10 TUES   Sex Pistols plus support band the Vibrators play the 100 club in London's Oxford Street.

13 FRI   Joe Strummer's new band the Clash announce their arrival to the press at their manager's rehearsal studio in Chalk Farm, North West London.

14 SAT   Birmingham, Barbarellas. Songs performed: 'Flowers of Romance'/'I Wanna Be Me'/'Liar'/'Substitute'/'Seventeen'/'New York'/'Steppin' Stone'/'No Fun'/'Satellite'/'No Feelings'/'Pretty Vacant'/ 'Problems'/'Anarchy In The UK' (**).

19 THUR   West Runton Village Inn near Cromer in Norfolk - the band turn up late.

21 SAT   Nottingham, Boat club.

The First European Punk Rock Festival takes place at Mont De Marsan in France with: Eddie & the Hot Rods, the Gorillas (**), the Pink Fairies, Nick Lowe, the Tyla Gang, Roogalator and the Damned. The Sex Pistols were booked to play but then banned by the promoters who think they have gone 'too far'.

29 SUN   The Clash play their first London gig at the Screen on the Green in Islington. The Sex Pistols headline and the Buzzcocks also play. The gig is an all-niter starting at midnight and lasting till dawn. I once read a list by a fan stating this was "Probably the Sex Pistols finest gig!!" Songs performed: 'Anarchy In The UK'/'I Wanna Be Me'/'Seventeen'/'New York'/'No Lip'/'Steppin' Stone'/'Satellite'/ 'Submission'/'Liar'/'No Feelings'/'Substitute' (**).

31 TUES   The 100 club, Oxford Street, London. Support bands are the Clash and the Suburban Studs. Songs performed: 'Anarchy In The UK'/'I Wanna Be Me'/'Seventeen'/'New York'/'No Lip'/'Steppin' Stone' /'Satellite'/'Submission'/'Liar'/'No Feelings'/'Substitute'/'Flowers Of Romance'/'Pretty Vacant'/'Problems'/'No Fun'/'Anarchy In The UK'/'I Wanna Be Me' (**).

EVENTS WHERE EXACT DATE IS UNKNOWN:

Sex Pistols record 'So It Goes' TV Show and perform 'Anarchy In The UK'. The show is screened on the 4th of September. 'Problems' was performed as a warm up number but almost certainly not recorded.

Sex Pistols play Middlesborough or Hartlepool in mid/late August.

PISTOLS in PRISON

Chelmsford maximum security prison isn't no council tenancy, but it is in the suburbs, right next to some office buildings and a service station on the corner (quick getaway). The prisoners are in for three years and up-weightlifting, join the film society for 11p a week, and, see rock bands (mostly recent releases), on acid—

"Oh, you mean Hawkwind?"

No, I mean the prisoners. Anyway, Hawkwind started yelling 'Kill! Kill!' and there was a minor riot. So no encores for them. Tonight it's the Pistols.

It was Paul's last day at the brewery, so he came down separately, walking through the front door, talk to the screw sitting behind a variety of chemicals. We are presenting walk through a noisy, dull grey sliding door into a small, dull grey room with a low ceiling, table with chair at each end, the door slides shut, instant claustrophobia, the metal grey door in front of him noisily slides open, walk into a puke green room and sit under the bulletin board—'Charlie Smith is having a leaving party (at his request) after 26 years of service. We are presenting him with a silver cup' wait for a screw to take you into the prison's innards. Upstairs in the mess, the band wait for Paul, sitting at a table devouring sandwiches and tea. John has dressed for the occasion: NO FUTURE FUTURE' down the front of his shirt, ANARCHY' dripping across the back.

Through the barred windows, across the courtyard, the rows of windows criss-crossed with three sets of bars, a cell block, the sun. At a table at the other end of the room a group of screws have afternoon tea, all blue & uniforms and golden in the afternoon belt, looping to their knee and ending in a fistful of keys. It really needs Godard, camera slowly tracking from one end of the room to the other, from Pistols to Police, to get the full effect.

Screw (incredulous): 'Is that the pop group?'

Other Screw (superior sneer): 'Well. They're supposed to be.'

The small theatre echoes a lot. There is a backdrop behind the equipment, a cityscape with lots of billboards, in between the Coke and Cinzano ads the simple messages POT and LSD. The band warm up with a diamond hard Wham Bam Thank You Maam', then a few of their own. When the sound check finishes everyone except sound wizards Dave and Kim have to go backstage, and the audience are let in.

They run. Long hair, short hair, young middle aged, their clothes a jumble of jackets, sweaters, slippers, boots. Six blacks stroll in; five of them walk out after ten minutes. Some guys have sewn flares into their levis.

"God, there won't be any girls in the audience," says Steve.

"That's alright," jeers Nils, "You'll still be able to play."

They walk on one by one. Steve gets a few wolf whistles. John gets a lot. He welcomes them with a greeting from the Queen (cheers and whistles) and a message from the recently released Ron, who would have loved to come, but he's been banned. Dead silence.

John enunciates 'Anarchy' very clearly. There is wild applause. 'I Wanna Be Me' gets a little less approval. There is a little less, and so on. And they are playing great. In the short breaks between songs John taunts them. You're like a bunch of fucking statues! I bet you've all got a good case of piles! Move!

"We're not allowed to."

I don't care—tear the fucking place apart!

The audience loves it, yelling back with no hesitation. They even warm to

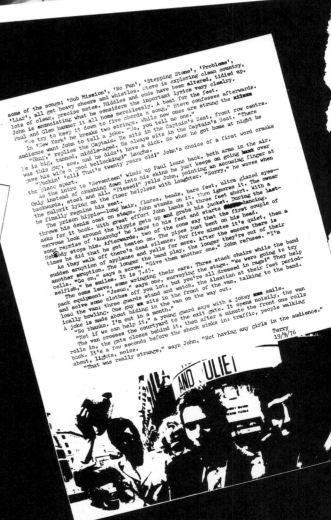

some of the songs; 'Sub Mission', 'No Fun', 'Stepping Stone', 'Problems', 'Liar', all get heavy cheers and whistles. Steve is exploring clean country, lots of clean, precise notes. Middles and ends have been altered, tidied up. John is enunciating what he considers the important lyrics very clearly. Paul and Glen hammer it all home mercilessly. A beat for the feet.

"We try to keep it down to five chords a song," Steve confesses afterwards. In New York he breaks two strings. "No, you tell me one are strung the audience want John to tell a joke. "No, you sit in the Captain's Seat, front row centre. He is big, tanned, middle-aged. He always sits in the Captain's Seat. "There was this guy, see, and he didn't have a dick. So when he got home at night he gave his wife a good bollocking!" Laughs.

"Juckin' 'ell! That's twenty years old!" John's choice of a first word cracks the place apart.

As the intro to 'Seventeen' winds up Paul leans back, both arms in the air. Only instead of crashing down into his skins he just keeps on going back over backwards, stool and all. "Pissed!" yells John, pointing an accusing finger at the culprit lying on the floor helpless with laughter. "Sorry," he waves when he finally regains his seat.

The prison hippie—long hair, flares, beads, bare feet, ultra glazed eyes—throws his denim coat on high. John stands on it, then ignores it. The owner asks for it back. With great effort John lands it three feet short. With a song reprise of 'Anarchy' he leaps to his feet and grabs his jacket. During the last nervous look around the hippie gets up and grabs his jacket. During the dancing, Nobody stops him. Afterwards, two of the cons say that the first couple of times he did that he got beaten on. The pipes just bent on his head.

As they walk off there's dead silence. For five minutes it's quiet, then a sudden eruption of applause and yells for more. After the encore there's a another eruption. The longer the band play, the longer they're out of their cells. "Go on," says a screw. "Give them another one." John refuses. "I'm selfish," he smiles. It is 7.45.

The cons leave, some wringing their ears. Three stack chairs while the band pack equipment. "Jesus," says one, surveying the stage. "We were going to try and active some clothes off you lot, but you're all dressed in rags!" They help load the van; three guards stand and watch, the Alsatian at their feet periodically howling. One guy sits in the front of the van, talking to the band.

A joke is made about hiding in the van on the way out.

"No thanks. I'm out in a month."

"Not if we can help it," a young guard says with a jokey smile, the van rolls in, a gate closes behind it, then after a minute the front one rolls back. It's a few seconds before the shock sinks in; traffic, people walking about, lights, noise.

"That was really strange," says John, "Not having any girls in the audience."

Terry
19/9/76

SEPTEMBER

NAGS HEAD, LONDON ROAD
HIGH WYCOMBE, BUCKS

SEX
PISTOLS

SUBURBAN STUDS
OPEN 7.30 TILL LATE: 70p ADM

1976

2 THUR   High Wycombe, Nags Head with support band the Suburban Studs. This was intended as a warm up gig for the Paris shows. Admission is 70p.

3 FRI   Sex Pistols, Malcolm and Crew fly to Paris. It's Steve's birthday, he gets a free glass of champagne from a stewardess on the plane, he was hoping for something more. When they arrive in Paris, Malcolm buys Steve a birthday present - a prostitute!

The Club De Chalet Du Lac, Paris in France. The club's opening night where many people turn up in expensive clothes. Unfortunately, some of the chairs are still wet from black paint. The band's first performance outside England. Siouxsie, Steve Severin, Billy Idol and one or two more fans drive over in Billy's ex-Post Office Morris van. Siouxsie wearing her usual outfit which includes a revealing cut-a-way bra manages to get molested. This is the first appearance of the so-called 'bondage suit'. Songs performed include 'Anarchy In The UK'/'I Wanna Be Me' and 'Seventeen'.

4 SAT   The band perform an afternoon show at the Club De Chalet Du Lac in Paris.

So It Goes TV programme is screened and shows the Sex Pistols performing 'Anarchy In The UK'.

5 SUN   Screen on the Green, Islington, in London?

11 SAT   New Musical Express runs a review of the Sex Pistols 'Screen on the Green' gig.

Whitby, Royal Ballroom.

12 SUN   Leeds, Fordgreen (Hotel?) Ballroom.

13 MON   Sophie Richmond begins employment as Malcolm McLaren's secretary, working out of his flat in Balham.

Sex Pistols play Chester, Quaintways.

15 WED   Blackburn, Lodestar.

17 FRI   Paul Cook finally quits his day job as an electrician's mate for a brewery.

Sex Pistols play a concert inside Chelmsford Maximum Security Prison for the prisoners. The concert is recorded by Dave Goodman on the mixing desk and the tape still exists to this day. Johnny really tries to 'wind-up' the members of the audience. They start with 'Anarchy In The UK' followed by 'I Wanna Be Me'/'Seventeen'/'New York'/'No Lip'/ 'Steppin' Stone'/'Satellite'/'Submission'/'Liar' (**).
They may also have played 'No Fun'/'Problems'/'Anarchy In The UK' and one more song as an encore. The show is over by 7.45pm.

20 MON   100 Club Punk Festival (first night) with Subway Sect, Suzie &
            the Banshees (**), the Clash (**). The Sex Pistols play:
'Anarchy In The UK'/'I Wanna Be Me'/'Seventeen'/'New York'/'No Lip'/
'Steppin' Stone'/'Satellite'/'Submission'/'Liar'/'No Feelings'/'Substitute'/
'Pretty Vacant'/'Problems'/'No Fun' and an encore of 'Anarchy In The
UK' (**). Tonight sees the live debuts of Subway Sect and Suzie
(thereafter 'Siouxsie') and the Banshees, the latter with Sid Vicious on
Drums. The Sex Pistols are paid £438 for their performance.

Sex Pistols sign to a five year management contract with Malcolm
McLaren's company, Glitterbest Ltd.

21 TUES   Second night of the 100 Club Punk Festival – Stinky Toys, the
            Damned, the Vibrators (later joined by Chris Spedding), the
Buzzcocks. Somebody smashes a glass during the Damned's set and a
fragment damages a young punk girl's eye. Sid Vicious is accused. Punk
is banned from the 100 Club.

Sex Pistols play Cardiff, Top Rank and receive £125.

22 WED   Sex Pistols play Swansea and are paid £125.

23 THUR   Newport scheduled but may have been cancelled? (Birkenhead?)

24 FRI   Burton upon Trent, 76 Club. Songs performed: 'Anarchy In The
            UK'/'I Wanna Be Me'/'Seventeen'/'New York'/'No Lip'/
'Steppin' Stone'/'Satellite'/'Submission'/'Liar'/'Substitute'/'No Feelings'/
'No Fun'/'Pretty Vacant'/'Problems' (**). This gig is later issued on a
bootleg record called 'Indecent Exposure' with 2 tracks missing 'No Lip'/
'Satellite'. It is also recorded through the mixing desk by Dave Goodman
(Sound Engineer/Producer). His tape is issued in 1985 as 'The Original
Pistols – Live'. This version includes 'No Lip' but excludes 'Steppin'
Stone'/'Satellite'/'Submission'. (note: 'Satellite' does not appear on
either release). The band are paid £136 for the gig.

27 MON   Doncaster, Outlook Club. They receive £134 for their
            performance. Nick Mobbs, head of A&R of EMI Records
            witnesses the band for the first time.

28 TUES   Guildford, The Place? (also listed as playing Bunters club?).

29 WED   Stoke, Strikes club.

30 THUR   Derby, Cleopatras. EMI witness the band's performance and
            decide to sign them. Contracts are exchanged eight days later
            (8th of October).

EVENTS WHERE EXACT DATE IS UNKNOWN:

Formation of Flowers Of Romance with Sid Vicious – Vocals, Steve Walsh –
    Guitar (later in Manicured Noise), Viv Albertine – Bass (later in the
    Slits), Palm Olive – Drums (also later in the Slits). They split up in
    February 1977 when Sid joined the Sex Pistols.

100 Club bans
punk bands

FOLLOWING THE outbreaks of violence at the 100 Club's two day punk rock festival last week (see Giovanni Dadomo's report in 'On the Road'), the club has stopped all future concerts involving punk bands.

Ron Watt who runs the club, said "There is a small faction that take what happens onstage too seriously. It's only a minority — but bad enough to stop any other similar performances in the immediate future.

"I want to stress that I don't blame any of the bands. They play out violence onstage and I think they're against it actually occuring.

"I am sorry to have to do this. I just hope that punk rock is not becoming synonymous with violence."

V.A.E.C. **STANDARD CONTRACT** as approved on 1st March 1976 by the VARIETY & ALLIED ENTERTAINMENTS' COUNCIL of Great Britain for Club, Cabaret & Variety Venue Engagements.

N.B. (i) CLAUSE 12 herein (Barring Clause) does not apply to the West End of London.

(ii) For ease of administration the Signatures to this Contract are placed between Clauses 1 and 2 but the Contract shall consist of Clauses 1 to 32 inclusive plus Schedule 1.

THIS CONTRACT is made the......**4th**............ day of ......**AUGUST**.............................19**76**...

between................**GREG VANDIKE**.................................(hereinafter called "the Management") of the one

part and...............**MALCOLM MCLAREN**.........................(hereinafter called "the Artiste") of the other part.

1.   The Management hereby engages the Artiste and the Artiste agrees to perform as per the following Schedule of Performances, as ......**Known**...(or in his usual entertainment), at the salary stated therein and subject to the undermentioned conditions provided that the salary paid under this Contract shall not be less than such minima as may be prescribed annually by the Variety & Allied Entertainments' Council. This Contract shall not be used for chorus.

SCHEDULE OF PERFORMANCES

Name of Act/Artiste...**SEX PISTOLS**...

Days & Dates of Engagement	Name & Full Postal Address of Venue	Time of Rehearsal	PERFORMANCES			
			No.	Times	Duration in Minutes	Salary per performance
Wed. Oct 6	Woods Club, Plymouth				1 x 60	80% Net Door Take
Cash on Night. Equipment to arrive 5.00 p.m.						

Commission : 10% to Endale   Total Salary.....................80%.........

Provided that

*(a)   For the purposes of calculating damages under Clause 29(ii) hereof the salary stated in the Schedule of Performances shall be deemed to be £............................. (being not more than three times the said salary).

*(b)   The Artiste is permitted to double at... under separate contract, which shall not be deemed a contravention of Clause 12 hereof, and on the understanding that such an arrangement shall not in any way prevent fulfilment of this Contract. Subject thereto the provisions of Clauses 10 and 11 shall prevail.

Not applicable unless completed and signed by both parties

S WITNESS the hands of the parties the day, month and year first above written.

r the Management..

ition Held :   *(Authorised Signatory)*

                                                       Member-Organisation **SEX PISTOLS**

ss, if different from that entered in Schedule of Performances   Sole representation and management:
                                                                          Malcolm McLaren
Artiste..   93 Bell Street, London, N.W.1.
                                                                          01-673 9855 · 01-723 ....*(Authorised Signatory)*
Number.....................................

not (delete whichever does not apply) registered for Value Added Tax.

V.A.T. Registration No. :........................

e of Artiste	Nationality	Permanent and/or Temporary Address
OLS		

gement hereby confirms and agrees to be responsible for the salary set out in the Schedule of Performances hereby undertakes to fulfil the said performances. In the event of this Contract being for the duration of thereof, the Artiste shall be paid forthwith upon the completion of the Contract and in the event of the nore than one week, the Artiste shall be paid on a weekly basis.

ols sign
ll deal

PISTOLS, the
h 'new wave'
been signed to

ar contract, with
r options and the
iday night and the
nt the weekend
single, 'Anarchy In
at the Lansdowne
release date has yet
but it is thought that
release the single
th.
ttle between the major
cord companies to sign
stols had hotted up over
fortnight. Every company
n the band and Polydor,
nd Chrysalis had all made

scooped the others by
ng up the fastest contract in
history — it was done in a
day — and by offering an
nce believed to be in the region
0,000, the largest amount ever
ed to an 'unknown' band.

The A&R manager of EMI, Nick
Mobbs, told SOUNDS this week:
"Here at last is a group with a bit of
guts for younger people to identify
with: a group that parents actually
won't tolerate. And it's not just
parents that need a little shaking
up; it's the music business itself.
"That's why a lot of A&R men
wouldn't sign the group; they took
it all too personally. But what other
group at a comparable point in
their career has created so much
excitement both on stage and off.
"For me the Sex Pistols are a
backlash against the 'nice little
band' syndrome and the general
stagnation of the music industry.
They've got to happen for all our
sakes.
The Sex Pistols begin a month-
long European tour next week
which will take them to Holland,
Belgium, France and Germany.
They will embark on a major UK
tour when they return which will
open at Manchester Palace Theatre
on November 20 and will include
their first appearance at a major
London venue.

1 FRI   Manchester, Didsbury College.

2 SAT   Johnny Rotton makes the front cover of New Musical Express and inside is a two page article including a review of the 100 Club Punk Festival.

5 TUES   Torquay, 400 Club (cancelled?).

6 WED   Plymouth, Woods Centre, scheduled but cancelled.

7 THUR   Penzance, Winter Gardens (cancelled?).

8 FRI   Sex Pistols are signed to EMI Records by Nick Mobbs, for a £40,000 advance. £20,000 payable on signing and a further £20,000 due October 1977. The contract is to run for two years with two one-year options. The royalty rate is 10% plus producer's royalty. The contract is said to have been drawn up, checked and signed by the evening of the same day. Chrysalis, RAK and Polydor (who have even paid for some studio time) have previously all made bids but Malcolm prefers EMI.

9 SAT   Northampton, Cricket Ground?

10 SUN   Sex Pistols are in Lansdowne Studios in Holland Park, West London recording a version of 'Anarchy In The UK' with Dave Goodman.

12 TUES   Dundee Technical College. Steve goes up in the van with the equipment and road crew while Paul, Glen & Johnny go up on the train. They stay in the same hotel as Frankie Vaughan! (they do not add 'Gimme the Moonlight' to their stage show!). A very good show, they play lots of encores!

13 WED   Wolverhampton, Lafayette club (possibly originally planned for the 8th but changed due to their signing with EMI on that date?).

14 THUR   Birkenhead, Mr Digby's?

15 FRI   Liverpool, Erics with support band the Yachts.

17 SUN   Sex Pistols go into Wessex studio with producer Chris Thomas and out of this session comes the version of 'Anarchy In The UK' that EMI release. A version of 'I Wanna Be Me' previously recorded and produced by Dave Goodman is used for the B side of the record.

18 MON   Throbbing Gristle supported by Chelsea (billed under the name 'LSD') play London ICA. The event is attended by amongst others, members of the so-called Bromley contingent and Mick Jones of the Clash.

20 WED   Birmingham, Bogarts. Songs performed: 'Anarchy In The UK'/ 'I Wanna Be Me'/'Seventeen'/'Satellite'/'Substitute'/'Liar'/'No Feelings'/'No Fun'/'Pretty Vacant' (**). Admission is 50p. The band arrive late at 9pm and appear on stage at 10pm.

21 THUR   A cheque for the first instalment of the EMI advance arrives – £20,000.

Dunstable, Queensway Hall supported by the Jam. Less than 80 people turn up. The Sex Pistols open with 'Anarchy In The UK'. The Jam appear as a four piece band Paul, Bruce and Rick plus a keyboard player. The Sex Pistols are paid £63.66.

22 FRI   Stiff Records release the Damned's 'New Rose' single – The first true UK punk record release and beating the Sex Pistols by about 4 weeks. The first shop in the World to actually stock the record is 'Remember Those Oldies' in Cambridge.

23 SAT   Sounds Newspage states; "Damned: first punx on wax" as their debut single is released. Jonh Ingham votes it 'Single of the Week'.

25 MON   Payment for the band's appearance on Granada TV's 'So It Goes' programme arrives in the morning post.

EVENTS WHERE EXACT DATE IS UNKNOWN:

They also play Scarborough and Derby? – details unknown.

At the beginning of October, Glitterbest Ltd (Malcolm McLaren's management company for the Sex Pistols) moves to 40 Dryden Chambers, 119 Oxford Street, London W1.

THE NASHVILLE ROOM

Thursday November 11th	Free
THE DERELICTS **+ THE VIBRATORS**	
Friday November 12th	
RING FOR DETAILS	75p
Saturday November 13th	
DARTS **+ TELEPHONE BILL & THE SMOOTH OPERATORS**	
Sunday November 14th	60p
CADO BELLE	
Monday November 15th	Free
MOVIES	
Tuesday November 16th	Free
PLUMMET AIRLINES	

CORNER CROMWELL ROAD/NORTH END ROAD, W14
(Adjacent West Kensington Tube)   Tel: 01-603 6071)

More punk news . . .

Meanwhile, the **SEX PISTOLS**, who recently signed a lucrative record contract with EMI and have their first single, 'Anarchy In The UK', (coupled with the Stooges' 'No fun') released on November 19, have fixed their first major London gig at no lesser venue than the Talk Of The Town on November 21. Tickets, price £2, go on sale at all the usual outlets from next Monday.

At the end of November the Sex Pistols will be going out on a British tour with another British act and two New York punk bands. And talks are now in progress over an American tour by the Pistols next Spring.

WE READ wit amusement a stor in another musi paper ruminatin on the rumours that the Se: **Pistols** had signed with EMI for £100,000. If they'd reac their SOUNDS they would already know it was for £40,000.

The Pistols have also been seeing a lot of poo-poo on the propellor since signing, with many claiming they've sold out. It should be pointed out that an advance is not a gift but a loan, which means that they're 40,000 quid in debt to the World's Safest Recording Company.

Ironically, EMI didn't want to release 'Anarchy In The UK' as a single, being worried about radio play. But with mucho arguing, hassling, and not having another finished track, the Pistols' anthem will be with us soon. Fighting the system from within may be viable, but it sure takes effort.

5 FRI   The Vibrators – 'We Vibrate' single is released on RAK label.

11 THUR   Recording 'Anarchy In The UK' for 'Nationwide' TV programme

12 FRI   Broadcast of 'Nationwide' including the Sex Pistols.

Chris Spedding & the Vibrators debut single 'Pogo Dancing' is released.

The Nashville Rooms, West Kensington, London is planned as a secret gig but cancelled at short notice.

13 SAT   Sounds announce a tour featuring the Sex Pistols, the Ramones, Chris Spedding + the Vibrators and Talking Heads.

15 MON   Notre Dame Hall, Leicester Place, off Leicester Square, London and the show is filmed for London Weekend Television. Some parts later used in the opening of "The Great Rock 'n' Roll Swindle". Songs performed: 'Anarchy In The UK'/'I Wanna Be Me'/'Seventeen'/'Pretty Vacant'/'No Feelings'/'No Lip'/'No Fun'/'Whatcha Gonna Do About It'/'Did You No Wrong'/'Seventeen'/'Steppin'Stone'/ 'Satellite'/'Problems'/'New York'/ 'Submission' (**).

(One of the versions of 'Seventeen' could be 'I'm A Lazy Sod' which some people think is a slightly different song with different words and was performed in the early days prior to being changed to 'Seventeen'? More likely is that Johnny forgets the words and makes some up). 4 tracks are later shown on London Weekend Television. Admission is £1.00. The band initially play a short set 'for the cameras' then play a 'real' set for the audience.

19 FRI   Hendon Polytechnic. First public performance of 'No Future'. Later the song title is changed to 'God Save The Queen'.

20 SAT   Manchester, Palace Theatre – planned but cancelled.

New Musical Express runs a news story that the Ramones have pulled out of the forthcoming co-headlined Sex Pistols tour. The bill now includes Chris Spedding & the Vibrators, the Damned, the Clash and from the USA – Johnny Thunders and the Heartbreakers.

SEX PISTOLS

OFF!

Straight in at 43 and moving up rapidly, so stock up while you've got the chance.

FIRST SINGLE
EMI 2566

PUNK TAKES

SOUNDS Star Single

SEX PISTOLS: 'Anarchy In The UK' (EMI). *Thrashing guitars, a maniacal chuckle from Johnny Rotten, and we're into the most eagerly-awaited single in ages. Single Of The Week? Has to be, and not just because Sounds was the first to feature the Pistols/Punk phenomenon. It explodes out of the pre-Christmas product pile, and by any standards it's a great rock record.*

In fact it has so many of the traditional ingredients of high-energy rock that it makes nonsense of all those hysterical letter-writers who see the Pistols as a threat to Music As We Know It. Conversely, it also makes nonsense of any claims that the Pistols are revolutionaries: they may want to push the old farts aside, but they've borrowed a lot from 'em.

Far from being bizarre, it's really a simple, basic record: so basic in fact that even fans of Hawkwind would feel at home with the relentlessly hammering rhythm section (shades of 'Silver Machine').

Pistols fans, I suspect, will be surprised (disappointed?) that the record isn't faster and nastier. It's just a little too smoothly produced Chris Thomas of Roxy Music fame. Will the Beeb ban it? Hard to see why: the opening line, 'I am an anti-Christ' is intended to shock, but in these irreligious times who can it offend?

No, this ain't revolution, it's the same old rock and roll — but YOUNGER and more intense than we've heard it for a long while. And as an old fart who loved the early Who, I welcome the Pistols.

ANARCHY IN THE U.K.
SEX PISTOLS

THE SUBWAY SECT I MEAN IT

Live La Résistance

THE Luscious Paul Cook

21 SUN   Talk Of The Town, London (planned but never played because the music press leak the story).

26 FRI   Sex Pistols 'Anarchy In The UK'/'I Wanna Be Me' (EMI 2566) single is released on EMI records. Originally the B side was going to be 'No Fun'. 5000 copies are issued in a plain black sleeve with both sides credited to Chris Thomas as producer. Dave Goodman threatened to serve an injunction on the record unless he is credited as producer of the B side and EMI respond immediately. From this moment on, all copies include the change and the record appears only in a normal EMI sleeve. Originally EMI were going to release the record on their 'Harvest' label (which issued Pink Floyd and Progressive Rock music in the early 1970's) but Malcolm told EMI in no uncertain terms that the Sex Pistols were not going to be put "on some bloody hippy label" and that they were signed to EMI and it must go out on the EMI label. To let you in on a little known secret – the backing track of 'Anarchy' is actually two separate rhythm tracks spliced together!

27 SAT   Sounds announces that the Vibrators have pulled out of the Sex Pistols forthcoming tour.

Sophie Richmond (Malcolm McLaren's secretary) starts to write her diary of events surrounding the Sex Pistols, these notes are later used to help compile the book 'The Sex Pistols – Inside Story' written by Fred & Judy Vermorel.

28 SUN   London Weekend Television screen a programme called "The London Weekend Show" on punk. It is only broadcast in the London area, starting at 1.15 pm. It includes snips of the Sex Pistols with live performances of 'Anarchy In The UK'/'Pretty Vacant'/ 'Submission' and 'No Fun' filmed at the Notre Dame Hall on the 15th.

29 MON   Sex Pistols play Coventry, Lanchester Polytechnic.

'Anarchy In The UK' sells 1765 copies today.

30 TUES   Even at this stage, Malcolm McLaren begins to wonder if EMI Records are really promoting 'Anarchy In The UK'. He has a meeting with Leslie Hill at EMI and is given reassurances.

Sales of 'Anarchy In The UK' for today are 1635 copies.

EVENTS WHERE EXACT DATE IS UNKNOWN:

Sex Pistols record some tracks at EMI's eight track studio at Manchester Square in London with Mike Thorne (who later produced Soft Cell). The tracks include 'No Future'/'Liar'/'Problems'/'Anarchy In The UK' and 'No Feelings'. 'No Feelings' possibly only got as far as the instrumental backing track?

During November Malcolm, Vivien, Jamie, et al put together the design of the 'Anarchy In The UK' magazine.

MIRROR COMMENT

Bleeps and the blame

THE faceless bosses of Thames Television must share the shame of red-faced Bill Grundy.

They deserve the rap because they knew well in advance that the Sex Pistols were likely to throw up a stream of verbal graffiti.

That's punk rock style.

London Weekend Television, who pre-recorded an interview with the group, had already bleeped out four-letter words.

Yet Thames chose to let Bill Grundy do the chat with these four-letter words-men LIVE

Such programmes, as the Independent Broadcasting Authority should insist, belong, at best, to late-late night viewing. With bleepers.

Not tea-time, with the children and Nan around.

Pistols tour chaos

THE SEX PISTOLS' first British tour was in tatters this week in the wake of a series of incidents which gave them front page headlines on the national newspapers for five consecutive days.

As SOUNDS went to press on Monday evening most of the tour dates had been cancelled or rearranged at alternative venues.

The remaining schedule now reads: Leeds University December 6, Manchester Electric Circus 9, Bristol University (formerly Colston Hall) 13, Caerphilly Castle Cinema (formerly at Cardiff) 14, Dundee Caird Hall 16, Guildford Civic Hall 19, Plymouth Woods Centre 21, London Roxy Theatre Harlesden 26.

However, the situation is constantly changing and fans should check with the venue before going.

An additional date in Croydon is being arranged for December 12.

The Pistols' Birmingham gig has been switched to the Bingley Hall and that at Torquay to Paignton Penelopes.

The Pistols were due to perform their show in front of the Derby Borough Council Leisure Committee last Saturday afternoon before a decision was made as to whether they would be allowed to play at the Kings Hall that evening.

The group were due to perform at 3.30pm and the place was awash with national newspaper reporters and cameramen as well as a large contingent of police outside in case of any rumoured demonstrations by the National Front or irate parents (neither demonstration happened).

But by 4.30pm the group had not arrived and councillor Shepley announced that the band had refused to appear at the preview unless the committee would also attend the show that evening. But the committee refused to agree and the show was cancelled. At one point it was suggested that the other groups on the tour — the Damned, the Clash and Heart Breakers — might appear without the Pistols but no sooner had the committee agreed than the managers of the other bands said that their groups would not appear without the Sex Pistols.

Bernard Rhodes, manager of the Clash said: "We don't agree to the terms we have to perform under. It's ludicrous that people who are 102 years old should be passing judgement."

The pistols remained at a hotel just outside Derby throughout the afternoon and later an EMI spokesman read out a statement from them which said: "The Sex Pistols feel that it is unreasonable to expect their performance to be judged by people unconnected with and unfamiliar with their music. They prefer to be judged by those who see their concerts and listen to their records.

On Sunday the group were involved in yet another incident when they uprooted potted plants in the foyer of a Leeds hotel and scattered them round the foyer as press photographers tried to take pictures of them.

THE Sun

Friday, December 3, 1976   5p   TODAY'S TV: PAGES 14 & 15

2-week ban on Grundy over 'filthy' show

SUN EXCLUSIVE

Miss World gets the brush-off home

PHILIPPA KENNEDY
...D will get the cold ...her government when ...to Jamaica for Christ-

...kspeare is an embarrass-...-wing Government who ...the anti-apartheid boy-...contest.
...steel bands — and none ...ceptions which normally ...hen she

WERE THE PISTOLS LOADED?

Punk Rock group 'plied with booze'

By MICHAEL GAY and BRIAN WESLEY

TV PRESENTER Bill Grundy has been suspended for two weeks over the four-letter words used by a pop group on his show.

The news came last night as the storm grew with a claim that the Punk Rock group involved, the Sex Pistols, were loaded with drink before going on the air.

Hundreds of viewers complained after the group used obscenities during an interview with Grundy on Thames TV's Today programme.

Mr Nits Stevenson, personal assistant to the group's manager Mr Malcolm McLaren, said they were given access to a liberal supply of drink first.

"They were left in a room for

Bill Grundy yesterday ... facing an inquiry.

an hour with all this booze," he claimed.

"There were people coming in every second. They were the boozing to get really drunk when they went out there."

He did not think the group "drove the booze for drinks ... "but I was bound to have had some effect."

Mr Stevenson said he did not see the interview but he understood the Sex Pistols were provoked into swearing.

A Thames TV spokesman denied that drinking turned up the group. He said: "It is the

WHY I DID IT
—See Page 5—

Miss World, Cindy Breakspeare, with fans at a London bingo hall yesterday.
PICTURE: ARTHUR EDWARDS

ROMP HOME IN BY-ELECTION
See Page 2

EMI TO DROP THE PISTOLS?

Now London's Roxy cancels punk gig

FOLLOWING THE Sex Pistols' controversial TV appearance last week EMI are debating whether to sever their connections with the group and their planned UK tour has been drastically reduced.

Answering a call by shareholders to end the Pistols' contract Sir John Reid, EMI Chairman said at a meeting last night (Tuesday): "They are the only punk rock group under direct recording contract to us.

"Whether EMI release any more of their records will have to be very carefully considered."

Told of the latest upset during their performance at Leeds, in which they insulted the Queen, Sir John added: "This will obviously influence the board decision on whether or not the contract was ended."

because of the group's behaviour and what they represent. They have rehearsed here and it has appeared in London, been brought to my attention that they have written all over the gentlemen's toilet walls. They're a joke. If they represent the music of '76 I'd rather close my theatre."

But a new punk venue — also called the Roxy — has appeared in London, in Neal Street, Covent Garden, which opens with a new band Generation X and Siouxsie Sue and the Banshees on December 14. It is hoped that the Pistols and the Damned

will play there at a New Year's Eve party.

Generation X play their first London gig on Friday at Central London Poly, and play the Hope and Anchor on December 22. The promoters of three dates by the Vibrators have pulled out because of the punk rock backlash.

Bass player Pat Collier said: "We are suffering the worst but we are not going to give in. There is nothing that the Establishment can do to stop punk coming through, but punk does not necessarily mean throwing glasses at people."

BILLY IDOL of Generation X

AT THE time of going to press the tour was as follows: Manchester Electric Circus December 9, Norwich 10, Liverpool Cavern 12, Dundee Caird Hall 16, Maidenhead Skindles Club 18, Guildford Civic Hall 19, Birmingham Bingley Hall 20, Plymouth Guildhall 21, Paignton Penelopes Ballroom 22, Plymouth Woods Centre 23.

Due to a constantly changing situation fans should check with the venue before going. Dates pulled out include Bristol (13), Aberdeen (14), and Glasgow (15). The latest cancellation is London's new rock centre the Roxy at Harlesden, manager Terry

THE NIGHT OF THE NASTIES

THE PUNK ROCK HORROR SHOW

By JOHN JACKSON

THE punk rock "nasties" who shocked millions of viewers with their filthy language came out with a fresh barrage of belches and obscenities last night.

The four, 19-year-old members of the Sex Pistols' group were unmoved by the criticism of their performance on Thames TV's teatime programme, Today.

They blamed it all on interviewer Bill Grundy.

"He was falling about all over the place," said leather-clad Steve Jones.

And the group's manager, 29-year-old Malcolm McLaren, claimed they had been "goaded" by the interviewer.

"They were set up for all this by Grundy," said Mr McLaren. They were goaded into saying lots of things that perhaps they did not intend to say.

"But there are no regrets. These lads were expressing the mood of most kids these days. They want a change of scene."

Manager McLaren

My boys were goaded says Sex Pistols' boss

"We do not need Rolls Royces and houses in the country. We can see all through that bull - -," Steve Jones refused to move nearer to Rotten for a photograph.

"He has got really smelly armpits," he said. The centre of Britain's notorious, new pop cult is a boutique called "Sex" in trendy King's Road, Chelsea.

Its owner, Vivienne Westwood is the girlfriend of the Sex Pistols manager Malcolm McLaren. They have lived together for ten years and have a nine-year-old son.

"There's nothing wrong with being nasty or rude," said 35-year-old Miss Westwood.

Belched

I asked if they accepted the description that they were boorish, ill-mannered, foul-mouthed, dirty, obnoxious and arrogant.

"No," said drummer Paul Cook. Alongside him, Glen Matlock belched.

"But they agreed that the publicity they had received could help the sale of their new single, Anarchy in the U.K.

"The kids in the street know what we are about and will put us in the charts," said the group's leader, Johnny Rotten.

Rotten, who has two safety pins through his right ear lobe, added, with another belch:

"Young people are trying to control their lives and the younger you are the less chance you have of being f - - - - - up."

She said viewers who complained about the Sex Pistols' TV performance were "hypocrites."

Amazed

"I was amazed that people can get so uptight about a word that is used constantly."

Leslie Hill, the managing director of EMI Records, who have backed the Sex Pistols with £40,000, also sprang to the group's defence.

"We deplore this type of incident but feel that in many cases it is deliberately provoked by the media," he said.

● DID YOU KNOW ?

WHEN rock star Elvis Presley first became famous, sponsors of TV shows in America refused to have him shown below the waist because the considered his act—below the waist anyway—was obscene.

THE SHOCKERS: punk rockers Steve Jones (left), Paul Cook, Johnny Rotten and Glen Matlock. Their filthy language on television outraged viewers

1 WED   Sex Pistols appear on London Weekend Television's 'Today'
               programme for what has become known as the infamous
'Grundy Interview'. This has been arranged by EMI because 'Queen' are
unable to appear and the TV producers are talked into the idea by Eric
Hall, a plugger in EMI's press office. The Sex Pistols were rehearsing at
the Roxy rehearsal centre at 8 Craven Park Road in Harlesden for their
forthcoming UK tour, when they are told of the arrangement. During the
interview Steve Jones uses the words 'fucking' and 'fucker' at
interviewer Bill Grundy, this causes a storm of controversy as hundreds
of people phone in to complain.

'Anarchy In The UK' sells 2435 copies in the shops today and that is
prior to the Bill Grundy incident that happens after they have closed!

Sid Vicious is in court for the glass throwing incident at the 100 Club
Punk Festival (September 21st).

2 THUR   Following on from the previous day's TV appearance, 'Anarchy
               In The UK' sells 1535 copies. A press conference is held at
EMI's Manchester Square offices with the band in attendance.

Virtually all the daily newspapers carry stories about the Sex Pistols
T.V. exploits from the previous evening. Proposed concerts at
Bournemouth, Preston, Lancaster, Newcastle and Norwich are cancelled by
the organisers due to the 'bad publicity'.

3 FRI   'The Sex Pistols single 'Anarchy In The UK' sells 1780 copies.

The 'Anarchy In The UK' tour is scheduled to start, but due to the Bill
Grundy interview and all the uproar caused by the daily newspapers,
most of the tour is being cancelled with each passing hour. The final
tour schedule just prior to the uproar is as follows:

FRI	3rd	NORWICH University	cancelled
SAT	4th	DERBY Kings Hall	cancelled
SUN	5th	NEWCASTLE City Hall	cancelled
MON	6th	LEEDS Polytechnic	PLAYED
TUE	7th	BOURNEMOUTH Village Bowl	cancelled
THU	9th	MANCHESTER Electric Circus	PLAYED
FRI	10th	LANCASTER University	cancelled
SAT	11th	LIVERPOOL Stadium	cancelled
MON	13th	BRISTOL Colston Hall	cancelled
TUE	14th	CARDIFF Top Rank	cancelled
WED	15th	GLASGOW Apollo	cancelled
THU	16th	DUNDEE Caird Hall	cancelled
FRI	17th	SHEFFIELD City Hall	cancelled
SAT	18th	SOUTHEND Kursaal	cancelled
SUN	19th	GUILDFORD Civic Hall	cancelled
MON	20th	BIRMINGHAM Town Hall	cancelled
TUE	21st	PLYMOUTH Woods Centre	PLAYED
WED	22nd	TORQUAY 400 Ballroom	cancelled
SUN	26th	LONDON Roxy Theatre, Harlesden	cancelled

Day File

TO   SIR JOHN E. READ

cc   L.G. Wood   6th December, 1976
      B. Samain

RE   SEX PISTOLS

Contract Date –	8th October, 1976
Advance –	£40,000 (recoupable) £20,000 paid £20,000 due October 1977
Contract Period –	2 years, plus two 1-year options
Royalty Rate –	10% plus producer's royalty
Recording Costs –	to be recoupable on royalties earned on sales

Future recording plans are to make a new single at the end of December for release in February, 1977. It is also planned to record an album in January for release in March/April.

We do in fact have two people travelling with them on the present tour. These are Mike Thorne from our A&R Department and Tom Nolan from the Press Office.

I have again checked on their behaviour as far as we are concerned. They are regarded as somewhat uncouth; however, they have been in this building on about ten days during the last three weeks, and there have been no problems of any kind.

Nick Mobbs feels that the violence aspect has been blown-up out of all proportion and that unfortunately some of the people who attend concert and club performances of so called "punk rock" do go looking for trouble which obviously rubs off on the performers. It is interesting that the reason for the cancellation of the concert in Derby on Saturday was due to the fact that the information produced suggested that fifty members of a motor-cycle club had made a block booking and were expected to cause trouble. In addition, it was also understood that the National Front were going to mount some sort of protest. On the recommendation of Paul Watts, therefore, the concert was cancelled. The press reports that it was cancelled because the Group would not perform before the Derby Town Councillors is therefore incorrect.

Cont/d

- 2 -

Regarding the supposed problems at the Dragon Noria Hotel in Leeds, I understand that the hotel was only concerned about the fact that there were so many press men in the lobby being a nuisance. In the absence of any of our representatives and indeed the Manager of the Group himself, the Group were asked to destroy a plant for the benefit of a Daily Express photographer. This they did and then paid the £25 cost of the plant to the hotel without any trouble of any kind.

Regarding the television performance on Thames, I understand that initially Thames wanted to have Queen on at very short notice, but as Queen were unavailable it was suggested that the Sex Pistols could do this instead. Eric Hall, who arranges this, in no way set-up what happened and indeed is personally extremely upset that his professional reputation with television producers etc may be affected by what happened.

I attach the sales figures to-date.

L. F. HILL

att.

News from EMI

ANNUAL GENERAL MEETING – 7 DECEMBER 1976

Comment on Content of Records by Sir John Read, Chairman

During the course of today's Annual General Meeting, Sir John Read, Chairman of the EMI Group said:

"The EMI Group of companies operates internationally and has been engaged in the recorded music business for over 75 years.

"During recent years in particular, the question of acceptable content of records has become increasingly difficult to resolve – largely due to the increasing degree of permissiveness accepted by Society as a whole, both in the UK and overseas. Throughout its history as a recording company, EMI has always sought to behave within contemporary limits of decency and good taste – taking into account not only the traditional rigid conventions of one section of Society, but also the increasingly liberal attitudes of other (perhaps larger) sections of Society at any given time.

"Today, there is in EMI's experience not only an overwhelming sense of permissiveness – as demonstrated by the content of books, newspapers and magazines, as well as records and films – but also a good deal of questioning by various sections of Society, both young and old, e.g. What is decent or in good taste compared to the attitudes of, say, 20 or even 10 years ago?

"It is against this present-day social background that EMI has to make value judgements about the content of records in particular. EMI has on a number of occasions taken steps totally to ban individual records, and similarly to ban record sleeves or posters or other promotional material which it believed would be offensive.

"The Sex Pistols incident, which started with a disgraceful interview given by this young pop group on Thames TV last week, has been followed by a vast amount of newspaper coverage in the last few days.

Cont'd

From the Group Public Relations Department
EMI Limited
20 Manchester Square London W1A 1ES

"Sex Pistols is a pop group devoted to a new form of music known as 'punk rock'. It was contracted for recording purposes by EMI Records Limited in October 1976 – ar unknown group offering some promise, in the view of our recording executives, like many other pop groups of different kinds that we have signed. In this context, it must be remembered that the recording industry has signed many pop groups, initially controversial, who have in the fullness of time become wholly acceptable and contributed greatly to the development of modern music.

"Sex Pistols have acquired a reputation for aggressive behaviour which they have certainly demonstrated in public. There is no excuse for this. Our recording company's experience of working with the group, however, is satisfactory.

"Sex Pistols is the only 'punk rock' group that EMI Records currently has under direct recording contract and whether EMI does in fact release any more of their records will have to be very carefully considered. I need hardly add that we shall do everything we can to restrain their public behaviour, although this is a matter over which we have no real control.

"Similarly, EMI will review its general guidelines regarding the content of pop records. Who is to decide what is objectionable or unobjectionable to the public at large today? When anyone sits down to consider seriously this problem, it will be found that there are widely differing attitudes between people of all ages and all walks of life as to what can be shown or spoken or sung.

"Our view within EMI is that we should seek to discourage records that are likely to give offence to the majority of people. In this context, changing public attitudes have to be taken into account.

"EMI should not set itself up as a public censor, but it does seek to encourage restraint.

"The Board of EMI certainly takes seriously the need to
to encourage the raising of standards

In the last few days before the tour, the concert at Lancaster University (10th) is banned and Preston Charter is added on that date but never played. After the mass cancellations, some gigs are quickly re-scheduled as follows: Bristol Colston Hall is changed to Bristol University and Cardiff changed to Caerphilly Castle Cinema. Croydon is provisionally added for the 12th. However, of these only Caerphilly on the 14th actually takes place. And in the final count, only 3 of the originally planned 19 concerts are ever played. They are Leeds (6th), Manchester (9th) and Plymouth (21st).

4 SAT Derby Borough Council Leisure Committee insist that the Sex Pistols must perform their show at a private meeting at 3.30 in the afternoon to decide if the performance is suitable for viewing, but the band refuse to turn up. The Clash and the Heartbreakers agree with this decision but the Damned say they are prepared to accept the Leisure Committee's terms. Malcolm McLaren and the band decide that this means the Damned must be asked to leave the tour after the Leeds show (6th).

5 SUN Sex Pistols are involved in an incident at the Dragonara Hotel in Leeds when some potted plants are uprooted in the foyer. Dave Goodman once told me that reporters from a national daily newspaper offered him £20 to throw some plants around.

6 MON EMI still have plans for the Sex Pistols to record a new single in late December for release in February 1977 and an album in January for release in March/April.

Leeds Polytechnic. This now becomes the 1st night of the 'Anarchy Tour' after the chaos and cancellations. Songs performed: 'Anarchy In The UK'/'I Wanna Be Me'/'Seventeen'/'Steppin' Stone'/'No Future (later called God Save The Queen'/'Substitute'/'No Feelings'/'Liar' (**). They also perform two encores 'Whatcha Gonna Do About It'/'No Fun'. The encores were not recorded. Support acts are the Clash, the Heartbreakers and the Damned. The Sex Pistols receive £698 for their performance. The Damned are asked to leave the tour after tonight's performance (see 4th).

7 TUES EMI hold their Annual General Meeting. The Sex Pistols and the content of their records plus the band's public behaviour are among of the main items on the agenda.

9 THUR Sex Pistols, the Buzzcocks, the Clash and the Heartbreakers play Manchester, Electric Circus. The Sex Pistols play 'Did You No Wrong'/'No Lip'/'Seventeen'/'Stepping Stone'/'No Feelings'/'New York'/'No Fun'/'Submission'/'Substitute'/'Problems'/'Satellite'/'Pretty Vacant' (**). The band are paid £500.

13 MON Talks are held to arrange a London show at the Rainbow.

14 TUES Sex Pistols play Caerphilly Castle Cinema and the local 'older generation' stage a demonstration against the concert including a prayer meeting and a speech by a local politician. The demo is filmed and excerpts are later shown in "The Great Rock'n'Roll Swindle". The band walk away with a £400 fee for their performance.

NATIONAL ROCK STAR

U.S., Canada 50c   DECEMBER 25, 1976   Price 12p

Aus. NZ. S.A. Rhod. 30c. Malta 12c. Malays $1.00.

SOUL MOVIE

STARSKY AND Hutch star David Soul comes crashing into the *RockStar* singles chart this issue at No. 16 — the highest new placing — in a week in which he has signed a major British film deal with Sir Lew Grade.

It is likely that the movies will be made in England, or a location based here.

The roles will be Soul's biggest in films to date although he featured in ''Magnum Force''.

Apart from his chart entry with ''Don't Give Up On Us'' Soul's current album also stands at No. 10 in the *RockStar* list.

A SINGLE, thought by many to be the original infamous ''C-Blues'' track by the Rolling Stones — coupled with ''Brown Sugar'' was released by Stiff Records this week.

The record has been sent out for private distribution by the company, which releases punk band The Damned plus Pink Fairies and Roogalator, but it is thought unlikely it will be made available to the public.

Stiff Records refused to comment on the controversial single, which was sent out with a covering letter and features a photograph of Mick Jagger.

They describe it as ''an obscure Argentinian single by some old hopefuls looking for a new record deal''.

Is it the Stones? *RockStar* singles reviewer Ian Flavin says yes and names the live ''Brown Sugar'' track as having been recorded live in LA, with Eric Clapton on lead.

Colleague David Hancock says no, and believes the single is a Stiff Records' promotion for a Stones sound-alike band being launched in '77.

It's a Rotten Xmas

We're bankrupt say the Sex Pistols

AS *ROCKSTAR* went to Press this week Sex Pistols' manager Malcolm McLaren announced that he and his lawyer had delivered a 48-hour ''Support the Sex Pistols or Else'' ultimatum to EMI.

Lead singer Johnny Rotten also phoned *Rock-Star's* Stephen Lavers to slam censorship against the band's single and said the Sex Pistols were now ''bankrupt'' as a result of the campaign against them and the cancellation of gigs. He added: ''We're sending begging letters''.

The Pistols backed the recent punk tour fiasco with their own money and are now understood to be faced with considerable bills.

ROCK STAR *ROD STEWART & BUT EXTRA DATE* | GENESIS RAINBOW

ALEX QUITS ROAD *Don't wanna crawl through walls no more*

AS EXCLUSIVELY reported in *RockStar* on November 13, Alex Harvey has given up one-nighters with SAHB and the band is to tour without him. Dates have now been announced and are on the news pages.

Quote from Elvis, Las Vegas, December:

''I UNDERSTAND plans are underway for a visit to London, and we hope we can do it real soon.''

ELVIS PRESLEY fan club secretary Todd Slaughter returned from a meeting with Colonel Tom Parker in Las Vegas this week and reported that — in spite of other incorrect reports, one of them in *RockStar* — Presley and Parker are now actively considering no less than eight offers to appear in Britain in 1978.

Elvis is fully booked for 1977 but Slaughter reports:

''It now seems possible that, after 20 years, Elvis will tour outside the U.S.

''In the past few months Parker has visited Canada, Australia and the Far East to discuss other offers.''

Slaughter considers a world tour a distinct possibility during 1978 but points out that any visit to Britain next year is out of the question.

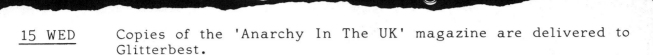
15 WED   Copies of the 'Anarchy In The UK' magazine are delivered to Glitterbest.

18 SAT   NME hold their Xmas Party at Dingwalls and among those grabbing the free food and drink are the Sex Pistols, the Clash, Eddie & the Hot Rods, the Damned, the Heartbreakers and the Flamin' Groovies.

19 SUN   Manchester, Electric Circus for the 2nd time in 10 days. The Sex Pistols receive £240.

20 MON   Cleethorpes, Winter Gardens. Songs performed: 'Anarchy In The UK'/'I Wanna Be Me'/'Steppin' Stone'/'Satellite'/'No Future'/'Substitute'/'Liar'/'No Feelings'/'Pretty Vacant' (**).
Tracie O'Keefe and Debbie (Wilson) Juvenile sell copies of the Anarchy In The UK magazine for the 1st time. Today's fee totals £200.

21 TUES   Sex Pistols, the Clash and the Heartbreakers play Plymouth, Woods Centre. About 300 people attend. They get £300.

22 WED   Sex Pistols plus the Clash and the Heartbreakers play a second night at Plymouth, Woods Centre. About 150 people turn up.

23 THUR   Ipswich, Manor Ballroom (planned but not played).

25 SAT/   The offices of Glitterbest (Sex Pistols management) are broken
26 SUN   into and a few items of little value are stolen.

27 MON   Sex Pistols are in the studio recording backing tracks.

EVENTS WHERE THE EXACT DATE IS UNKNOWN:

Sid Vicious is interviewed by 'Skum' fanzine.

The losses of the Anarchy tour are estimated at £10,000.

News from EMI

6th January 1977

EMI AND THE SEX PISTOLS

EMI and the Sex Pistols group have mutually agreed to terminate their recording contract.

EMI feels it is unable to promote this group's records internationally in view of the adverse publicity which has been generated over the last two months, although recent press reports of the behaviour of the Sex Pistols appear to have been exaggerated.

The termination of this contract with the Sex Pistols does not in any way affect EMI's intention to remain active in all areas of the music business.

*

Enquiries: Rachel

Group F

01-486

*   *

EMI and Pistols bid final farewell

THE SEX PISTOLS and EMI have now officially terminated their contract, despite last week's statement from Pistols' manager Malcolm McLaren in which he claimed that the band had no intention of being bought off by the record company.

The settlement involved EMI paying the Pistols the remainder of their £40,000 advance, a figure agreed upon shortly before Christmas when the band originally signed the contract.

McLaren this week attacked shop floor members of EMI for their lack of support for the band.

"I'm a bit disappointed in the people working within the recording industry. They seem a bit spineless," he said.

"I didn't want to see the contract ended, but I had no alternative because no-one at EMI was willing to work with us. I was hoping that the band would get some support from the people they worked with.

"At the moment we're just sitting down and trying to work out what to do. We have signed with no other record company, and we are only prepared to sign a contract that will prevent this sort of thing happening again.

"Finding a contract like that isn't going to be easy."

A prepared statement from EMI records read: "In accordance with the previously stated wishes of both parties and the verbal telephone agreement of Thursday January 6, documents terminating the contract between EMI and the Sex Pistols have now been agreed.

"EMI Records wish the Sex Pistols every success with their next recording contract."

THE BUZZCOCKS, the Manchester new wave band, are releasing a single on their own New Hormone label at the end of January.

Titled 'Spiral Scratch', the record will consist of four songs — 'Breakdown', 'Time's Up', 'Boredom' and 'Friends Of Mine' — and will sell for £1. A distribution deal is currently being negotiated.

From the Group Public Relations Department
EMI Limited
20 Manchester Square London W1A 1ES

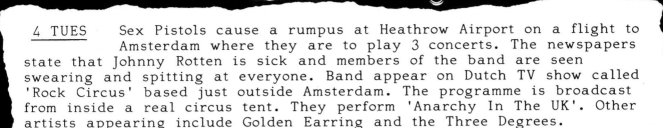

<u>4 TUES</u>   Sex Pistols cause a rumpus at Heathrow Airport on a flight to Amsterdam where they are to play 3 concerts. The newspapers state that Johnny Rotten is sick and members of the band are seen swearing and spitting at everyone. Band appear on Dutch TV show called 'Rock Circus' based just outside Amsterdam. The programme is broadcast from inside a real circus tent. They perform 'Anarchy In The UK'. Other artists appearing include Golden Earring and the Three Degrees.

<u>5 WED</u>   Paradiso Club, Amsterdam: 'Anarchy In The UK'/'I Wanna Be Me'/'Seventeen'/'New York'/'Satellite'/'God Save The Queen'/ 'Substitute'/'No Feelings'/'Pretty Vacant'/'Liar'/'Problems' (**).

<u>6 THUR</u>   Sex Pistols play Rotterdam, Art Centre.

EMI issue a press release and allege that their contract with the Sex Pistols has been mutually terminated by a verbal telephone agreement.

<u>7 FRI</u>   Paradiso Club in Amsterdam for 2nd time (see 5th). Glen Matlock plays his last ever live show with the Sex Pistols.

<u>8 SAT</u>   Sex Pistols and Malcolm McLaren return to London.

<u>9 SUN</u>   Secret negotiations start between Malcolm McLaren and A&M records. RCA, WEA and CBS show interest.

<u>12 WED</u>   Johnny Rotten is arrested for possession of 'Speed'.

<u>15 SAT</u>   It is announced that 'Anarchy In The UK' has sold 55,000 copies before being withdrawn by EMI records. It receives only 5 plays on the radio and is released in Britain, Belgium, Germany, Holland and Australia by EMI or its associated companies.

<u>17 MON-</u>   Sex Pistols in Gooseberry recording studio with Dave Goodman
<u>20 THUR</u>   and lay down 6 tracks: 'No Future'/'Problems'/'Pretty Vacant' /'Liar'/'EMI'/'New York'.

<u>22 SAT</u>   EMI Records officially terminate the Sex Pistols recording contract in writing. The band receive £30,000 (£20,000 being the unpaid balance of their £40,000 advance) plus £10,000 from their publishing contract with EMI. With the passing of time it seems that one of the main reasons the band were dropped is because of the association between EMI and Thames Television (EMI has a 50% share in Thames).

<u>24 MON</u>   Sex Pistols finish the recording of 6 tracks started on the 17th. While in the studio, CBS TV send down a film crew and the band are filmed miming to 'New York'.

<u>26 WED</u>   Band in the recording studio.

<u>28 FRI</u>   Dave Goodman mixes the 6 tracks recorded at Gooseberry studio in Eden studio, Chiswick.

<u>31 MON</u>   Birthday of Johnny Rotten, born this day 1956.

Pistols sack bassist

SEX PISTOLS' bassist Glenn Matlock has left the group and has been replaced by Sid Vicious.

Pistols' manager Malcolm MacLaren told SOUNDS this week that Glenn had left the group over 'irreconcileable musical differences'. The band had asked him to leave and replaced him with Sid.

"Sid's always been a close friend of the band and now he can play bass very well," added Malcolm. "The change has been in the air since Christmas."

Matlock apparently remains good friends with the rest of the band and will be getting his own group together shortly.

MacLaren added that the Pistols would be signing a new record contract, following their departure from EMI, at the end of this week. The band have been rehearsing with the new line-up and will be going into the studio this weekend to lay down some album tracks. A new single is expected later this month.

A European tour is being set for April but there are no British plans at present as the problems of finding suitable venues for them have still not been resolved.

PISTOLS LATEST

SEX PISTOLS have decided not to go ahead with their projected European tour, originally planned to run from this week until February 24. A spokesman for the group explained: "We decided it was rather pointless when they don't have a record to promote. And in any case, it would not have been financially viable. The Pistols feel they would rather remain in Britain to await a new recording deal".

Manager Malcolm McLaren is currently having discussions with several major labels, and the spokesman added that he is hopeful about a new contract being signed shortly.

PISTOL QUITS

SEX PISTOLS' bass guitarist, Glen Matlock, has quit the band following a personality clash with Johnny Rotten.

The rift, still officially denied by the Sex Pistols' management, has been growing since the band's controversial tour late last year.

"I've been getting a load of needle for ages, and since the tour I knew it wouldn't last. It was mainly friction between me and Johnny. On stage he's great but he'd carry all that into the rehearsal situation and I couldn't handle it," commented Matlock.

"There was no working relationship, especially as I'd always felt that he was putting it on. He'd put up this front."

Matlock, who had been with the Sex Pistols since their first live gigs in January last year, is now forming a new band with Jimmy Norton, a friend from St Martin's Art College in London. The working name is Rich Kids.

The Pistols' office, meanwhile, have yet to confirm Matlock's departure from the band. Sid Vicious, however, is believed to be his replacement.

MEMBERSHIP CARD

The ROXY

41-43, NEAL STREET, COVENT GARDEN, W.C.2.

Name.............. ....

Date of expirey................................. No...........................

Signature ....

1 TUES		Glen Matlock buys a secondhand car, it's a blue Sunbeam Alpine.
4 FRI		Talk of Sid Vicious taking Glen Matlock's place in the Sex Pistols.
11 FRI		Sid Vicious is auditioned for the job of bass player at the band's rehearsal room at 6 Denmark Street.
13 SUN		Malcolm McLaren flies to Los Angeles for talks with A&M Records.
16 WED		The Vibrators play the Roxy club. Members of the audience included: Three Sex Pistols, Cherry Vanilla and rumoured to be there, Mick Jagger!
18 FRI		Sid Vicious passes his audition and is rehearsing with the Sex Pistols.
19 SAT		Malcolm McLaren agrees to a tour of Finland organised by Miles Copeland.

Sounds 1977 Readers Poll produces the following results: Anarchy In The UK is voted 8th best single. It is also voted No 1 worst single. Eddie & The Hot Rods are voted No 1 Best New band and the Sex Pistols poll 10th place and Rat Scabies is voted 10th best Drummer.

NME 1977 readers Poll includes: Most Promising Emergent Act: No 1 – Eddie & The Hot Rods, No 6 – Sex Pistols, No 15 – The Stranglers. Best Group: No 11 – Eddie & The Hot Rods. Best Single: No 4 – Anarchy In The UK. Most Wonderful Human Being: No 1 – Johnny Rotten.

20 SUN	Malcolm McLaren returns from Los Angeles.
24 THUR	Glen Matlock leaves the Sex Pistols, the band say he has been sacked, he says he had already decided to leave!

The Clash sign to CBS Records.

25 FRI	Malcolm McLaren changes his mind about the proposed tour of Finland.

EVENTS WHERE EXACT DATE IS UNKNOWN:

Rumours are heard that the Sex Pistols have signed to RCA records.

From mid-February Malcolm has talks with CBS Records.

Melody Maker

MARCH 26, 1977   15p weekly   USA 75 cents

ROTTEN: ● They've given us up through fear and business pressure. They've kicked us in the teeth. We mean what we say. A record company is there to market records —not dictate terms ●

FIRING OF PISTOLS —TURN TO PAGE 3

NEWS STORIES

Week ending 19 March 1977

PISTOLS CONTRACT TERMINATED

A&M Records wishes to announce that its recording agreement with the Sex Pistols has been terminated with immediate effect. The company therefore will not be releasing any product from the group and has no further association with them.

<u>26 SAT</u>   Melody Maker's front cover quotes Johnny Rotten as saying "They've given us up through fear and business pressure. They've kicked us in the teeth. We mean what we say. A record company is there to market records – not dictate terms".

<u>28 MON</u>   Sex Pistols return to the UK from Berlin.

<u>EVENTS WHERE EXACT DATE IS UNKNOWN:</u>

Glen Matlock forms his band the Rich Kids with Steve New on guitar and Rusty Egan on drums. Midge Ure joins later as vocalist/guitarist. They play 4 or 5 low key gigs with Mick Jones (from the Clash) including the Brecknock and the Vortex. The Vortex was recorded and exists on a bootleg tape. Glen asks Paul Weller (of 'The Jam') to join but he declines the offer.

Johnny Rotten is fined £40 for possession of amphetamine sulphate by Marlborough Street magistrates. Rotten claims that he earns £25 per week of which he gives £15 to his mother for his keep.

25,000 copies of the Sex Pistols single – God Save The Queen are manufactured for the A&M record label at the CBS pressing plant in Aylesbury. Most copies are then destroyed after the Sex Pistols are fired from the label. A few copies survive and at the time of writing (1988) are changing hands for between £250 and £300 per copy.

Dave Goodman, the original Sex Pistols producer and sound engineer starts 'The Label' and issues a record by Eater titled 'Outside View'.

SOUNDS March 19 1977 15p

SEX PISTOLS SIGN FOR £150,000

sounds

**Next single:
'God Save
The Queen'
— story
inside**

SEX PISTOLS outside Buckingham Palace where they signed a £150,000 contract with A and M Records. From left: Johnny Rotten, Steve Jones, Paul Cook and new man Sid Vicious.

Evening Standard

47,350.

London: Thursday March 17, 1977   7RR   7p

Sacked again—but Pistols get £75,000

By Stephen Clackson

PUNK rockers the Sex Pistols have been sacked again—only seven days after signing with a new record company.

Manager Malcolm MacLaren walked out of the Chelsea offices of A & M Records early today with a terminated contract in one hand and a pay-off cheque for £25,000 in the other. He was paid £50,000 when the group signed up last week.

A & M were unwilling to expand on the reasons for their dramatic change of heart over the Sex Pistols this morning.

Managing Director Derek Green, who only last week so enthusiastic about them, was not in his office today and other executives were not to be tempted into discussing the affair.

MacLaren says that A & M told him there was dissension within the company over the Sex Pistols, that they were being subjected to "industrial blackmail" and other artists with the company disliked the idea of sharing a record label with the punk rockers.

They had also decided, he claims, that they didn't like the group's image any more.

A & M Records issued a brief statement early today saying that the Sex Pistols' recording contract, valued at £150,000 and guaranteeing 36 records, had been terminated "with immediate effect."

Spokesman Kit Buckler said: "The company will not be re-

leasing any product from the group and has no further association with them."

A & M signed the notorious group up a week ago and planned to issue a new record next month — God Save The Queen next month. Twenty thousand copies have been produced and the group will now try to get them and perhaps arrange alternative distribution.

When the Sex Pistols were

dropped by EMI in January because of their public behaviour, the cancelled contract earned them £50,000.

Today MacLaren said: "I'm shellshocked. Four weeks ago I flew to Los Angeles to meet Herb Alpert and Gerry Moss, who head A & M, and a week ago we signed up.

"They knew what they were getting and managing director Derek Green even said that he

wasn't offended by the group's behaviour and that he thought they were fresh and exciting.

"Then at 11.30 last night I got a telex from them saying it was all over.

"The Sex Pistols are like some contagious disease—untouchable.

"I keep walking in and out of offices being given cheques. When I'm older and people

ask me what I used to do for a living I shall have to say: 'I went in and out of doors getting paid for it.' It's crazy."

The Sex Pistols were sacked by EMI after releasing only one record Anarchy In The UK with the company. The four-man group had received £30,000 as a signing-on fee in the autumn and got £20,000 termination settlement of contract

Blue Angel

THE PAY-OFF — Malcolm MacLaren with A & M's cheque for £25,000 today. With him Sex Pistols, from left: Steve Jones, Sid Vicious, Johnny Rotten and Paul Cook.

Evening Standard : Richard Young

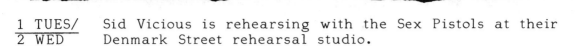

1 TUES/   Sid Vicious is rehearsing with the Sex Pistols at their
2 WED   Denmark Street rehearsal studio.

3 THUR/   Sex Pistols are in the recording studio with producer
4 FRI   Chris Thomas. Steve Jones plays the Bass guitar parts.

5 SAT   Sex Pistols play Notre Dame Hall, London. This is not a
          public show but just for an American TV company?

9 WED   Sex Pistols sign to A&M – the 'real' contract that is (see
          following story).

10 THUR   Sex Pistols sign a recording contract with A&M Records outside
          Buckingham Palace. The band get £150,000 (over two years)
and the contract calls for 18 songs to be recorded per year for two
years. The "proper" signing of contracts took place the previous
afternoon (9th) at the offices of Rondor Music.

11 FRI   Johnny Rotten appears in court on the charge of possession of
          'Speed'. He is fined £40.

12 SAT   In the early hours of the morning, members of the Sex Pistols
          and their entourage are involved in a scuffle with DJ Bob
Harris of the 'Old Grey Whistle Test' TV programme at the Speakeasy club
in London.

16 WED   Malcolm McLaren attends a meeting with A&M Records and they
          terminate the recording contract. The Sex Pistols are paid
£25,000 compensation. Malcolm later quips "I keep walking in and out of
offices being given cheques" (£50,000 had already been paid upon the
band signing just seven days before).

18 FRI   Malcolm has talks with CBS Records.

White Riot, the debut single by the Clash is released on CBS Records.

21 MON   Sex Pistols play London's Notre Dame Hall and it is filmed by
          the American NBC TV company. They play 11 songs including:
'God Save The Queen'/'I Wanna Be Me'/'Seventeen'/'Pretty Vacant'/'EMI'/
'Problems'/'No Feelings'/'Anarchy In The UK'.

22 TUES   The date that Glen Matlock 'officially' leaves the Sex Pistols
          with legal documents agreed and signed. He receives a
          payment (£2000?) in lieu of royalties.

The Sex Pistols fly to Jersey to "try and get away from it all".

23 WED   The Sex Pistols are ordered to leave Jersey.

24 THUR   The band fly to Berlin in Germany for a holiday.

25 FRI   The scheduled date for A&M to release 'God Save The Queen'
          but they were sacked from the label on the 16th.

Scen on the green

Sex Pistols
London

IN WHICH it must be conceded that Malcolm McLaren has a first class media brain with a perfect instinct for theatre.

He can now have his cake and eat it — the media hype around the Pistols is so entangled that people will now believe anything. Always there are two or three different explanations for any given event or stroke pulled.

So, it isn't quite as simple as a band playing. Tonite, a fine set notwithstanding, theatre ruled. The Notre Dame incident was a good taster for the 'entrance game' — get in round the front, no, round the side, no, round the back, maybe I'll be shut out. Instant aristocracy — people fight to get in. And only the converted (or very curious) come to Islington on a Sunday nite. But it is, at least, free.

After a longish wait, the audience of 350 get to watch a home movie collage of Pistol happenings — swinging London camp (Young Nation), gigs, councillors, Derek Nimmo at Sex 'So It Goes' and the Grundy event. It's disturbing, cheap and nasty: the sight of Rotten filling the screen is chilling (someone's been watching 'Privilige'). McLaren's shop gets plugged, the straight media is fooled, ritual bogey figures are there to be hissed at (press button). Us and them.

The Slits support — no competition. The fact they are an all-girl band and that's great wears off into a headache after two numbers. But their musical ineptitude doesn't matter — they are a great SHOW — having increasing presence and style as trash. Ari kicks a cymbal over/tempers flare — the circus bays for more.

More waiting, frustration and boredom. A good atmosphere for the Pistols to operate in. They've improved since last November. Even tho' the material is familiar — 11 songs plus two encores, the only newish material being 'EMI' and 'No Future'. In fact, they seem frozen in time: Rotten still berates the audience and slams drinks — not quite so whole-heartedly. It's only the rarity of gigs that allows them to stay still. Musically — Cook is the base, Jones runs through his guitar hero routines — Vicious stands legs astride, playing adequately, but he looks the part. Rotten is totally mesmeric: The lurker in derelict alleys, a spastic pantomime villain, with evil for real.

By now, to the audience, musical and stylistic consider-ations are all but irrelevant. The Pistols have become symbols — us against them — the songs anthems, inviolate from criticism. Just to see them is enough — it's a bonus that they played a good set.

So ultimately, the environment was totally controlled in favour of the Pistols — no risks. I admire the media manipulation, but feel the sour taste of patronage and the exploitation of base brutality instincts. It's too easy — the eventual problem may be — who cares?

They're being overtaken. Fast.
— JON SAVAGE.

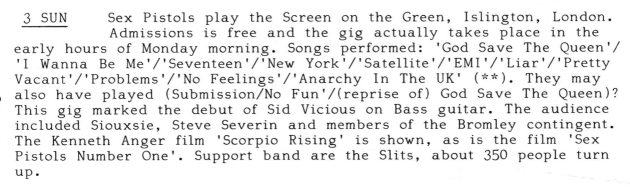

3 SUN   Sex Pistols play the Screen on the Green, Islington, London.
         Admissions is free and the gig actually takes place in the
early hours of Monday morning. Songs performed: 'God Save The Queen'/
'I Wanna Be Me'/'Seventeen'/'New York'/'Satellite'/'EMI'/'Liar'/'Pretty
Vacant'/'Problems'/'No Feelings'/'Anarchy In The UK' (**). They may
also have played (Submission/No Fun'/(reprise of) God Save The Queen)?
This gig marked the debut of Sid Vicious on Bass guitar. The audience
included Siouxsie, Steve Severin and members of the Bromley contingent.
The Kenneth Anger film 'Scorpio Rising' is shown, as is the film 'Sex
Pistols Number One'. Support band are the Slits, about 350 people turn
up.

4 MON   Malcolm McLaren contacts five record companies regarding a
         recording contract for the Sex Pistols but they all turn down
         his offer.

6 WED   Sid Vicious is ill, he has Hepatitis!

9 SAT   The 'Jaws' page of Sounds includes a photo of Johnny Rotten
         tied to a cross, The caption reads: "What A Way To Spend
         Easter Dept".

14 THUR Sex Pistols spend much of the day at Malcolm's shop trying
         on clothes in a photo session for Bravo (German magazine).

15 FRI   Malcolm is busy working on the proposed Sex Pistols film!

16 SAT   Sid Vicious goes into Hospital for treatment of Hepatitis.

22 FRI   Polydor, who have been interested in signing the Sex Pistols
         since 1976 decide to drop out of the running and not offer the
         band a contract.

25 MON/26 TUES   Sex Pistols (minus Sid) in Wessex recording studio.

EVENTS WHERE EXACT DATE IS UNKNOWN:

The Damned become the first UK Punks to play in America!

During April Malcolm is constantly being phoned by Richard Branson but
     he doesn't really want to sign with Virgin.

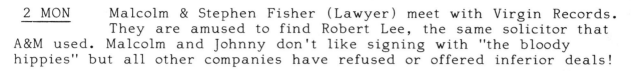

2 MON   Malcolm & Stephen Fisher (Lawyer) meet with Virgin Records. They are amused to find Robert Lee, the same solicitor that A&M used. Malcolm and Johnny don't like signing with "the bloody hippies" but all other companies have refused or offered inferior deals!

6 FRI   Sex Pistols sign to Barclay records for France, Switzerland, Zanzibar and Algeria for £26,000. The deal is for two years.

Sex Pistols are in the recording studio. Steve Jones is busy laying down guitar parts for 'New York'.

9 MON   Johnny Rotten receives a Tax Demand for £18,000!

10 TUES   Birthday of Sid Vicious of the Sex Pistols born this day 1957.

13 FRI   Three members of the Sex Pistols sign to Virgin Records (Sid is in hospital and signs on the 16th). Malcolm McLaren had approached Virgin in 1976 before they signed with EMI but Virgin were not interested at that time and turned him down flat. They receive £15,000. Later in the day Sid Vicious comes out of Hospital.

16 MON   Sid Vicious signs his part of the Sex Pistols contract with Virgin Records (the other 3 members signed on the 13th when Sid was in hospital).

17 TUES   CBS Records whose pressing plant in Aylesbury manufactures records for Virgin refuse to press copies of 'God Save The Queen', and talk of going on strike. But in the end it is all sorted out.

18 WED   Platemakers refuse to make plates for record sleeves.

Malcolm is interviewed on LBC Radio, London.

21 SAT   New Musical Express includes an advert placed by Glitterbest for the sale of Sex Pistols T-Shirts at £3.50 each.

23 MON   Sex Pistols sign an agreement with Cowbell Agency for them to handle the band's live bookings.

24 TUES   On this bright Tuesday afternoon, while taking part in a photo session arranged by Virgin records for promotion of the 'God Save The Queen' single, members of the Sex Pistols are stopped and searched by a policeman in Portobello Road. No charges are brought.

26 THUR   The band, Malcolm, and assorted followers go to Paris for the showing of a short Sex Pistols film edited by Julian Temple. While there, Malcolm visits Folies Bergeres as a possible place for the band to play.

Sex Pistols single 'God Save The Queen' goes on sale at Remember Those Oldies in Cambridge after they have Virgin send 200 copies by express delivery. Possibly the first shop in the World to actually sell the record?

The Sex Pistols wouldn't talk to us this week (sob!), so instead
we bring you this heart-warming exclusive interview
from the Islington Gazette...

JAWS

Why the X-certificate superstar is still mother's pride

ISLINGTON GAZETTE FRIDAY MAY 27 1977 - THIRT

Johnny's top of the pops with me says Mrs Rotten

By Robert Eddison

THE SEX PISTOLS could have no stauncher ally than Johnny Rotten's mum.

Which is just as well because, with punk rock storming back into the news again, they're going to need all the support they can get against the growing army of "Disgusteds."

"I wanna riot! Fans smash 200 seats at Punk Show" screamed a recent Evening Standard headline after London's largest-ever new wave punk rock concert.

It was The Clash group that night. The Sex Pistols have been in limbo for a while, following the bans provoked by their earthy language on television.

For months now, Eileen Lydon's anger at her son's treatment has been simmering just below the surface. But in an exclusive interview with the Gazette at her home on the Six Acres Estate, Finsbury Park, Johnny's sharp-shooting mum fired off enough verbal salvoes to bring down a whole army of punk-stopping councillors.

"Surely it's better to let out your anger with a few swear words than with violence?" blazed this Irish-born mother of four.

"On that 'Today' programme, if they'd wrecked the studios and everyone in them, they could hardly have been worse treated.

"It's true I've brought up my children to be plain-speaking. OK, so Johnny will sometimes say things straight from the shoulder, but he's not the violent type at all.

"Yet, he seems to bring out violence in others. One viewer got so worked up at their language that he swore back at them and kicked in his colour TV set, the stupid nut.

"I hate those punk rockers, people say to me. 'They're so violent.' Yet, they're NOT violent. It's the anti-punks who are the real troublemakers. There wasn't any trouble at the Screen On The Green concert; they were all our own followers in that audience."

She handed me a steaming mug of tea with HANDS OFF! painted round the side. There was an ominous silence. After the scatter fire, you could almost hear the big guns being mobilised.

"I can understand people being shocked at something new. But that's no reason, sod it, for the press to invent stories about my son's group vomiting all over Heathrow airport and spitting at the air staff. They were even supposed to have done something the press 'couldn't write about.' Can you imagine?

"How disgusting!', people say, 'to stick pins through their ears and nose.' What the hell has it got to do with them? It's THEIR nose and ears, isn't it?

"In fact," confided Eileen, leaning forward on the divan, "they don't stick them right through. It just looks that way."

The phone rang. For Johnny, of course. From some girl in Manchester who wouldn't leave her name. With him out so much, mum fielded the calls on automatic, like a human answering machine.

"People take them so seriously," she went on, ignoring the interruption.

Many's the laugh Johnny and I have over it. Being both Aquarius, we have the same sense of humour.

"There was this vicar, I remember, marching up and down in the snow outside the Welsh Hall they'd booked for a concert. 'Keep out of there!', he shouted. 'They're the Devil's Children!'

"There are more nutters outside than in, if you ask me. He must have heard their banned single: 'Anarchy In The UK,' where Johnny sings 'I'm An Anti-Christ.' Fancy him believing it was true! He's the Anti-Christ if anyone is. His job, after all, is to save everyone."

And that little matter of the drugs charge?

"Pop stars get handed all sorts of things after concerts. They can't examine everything their fans give them. Besides, it was only Speed: it wasn't a hard drug. When I went along to the West End Central police station to bail him out, I went mad at the way they treated him — like a common criminal.

"My boy is doing his own thing. He's not going around murdering people," she shot out. "In fact, groups like Johnny's help society by bringing kids in off the

streets. A friend of ours thinks the Sex Pistols are doing more good for the country than Jim Callaghan."

A budgie flew past and landed on the teapot. The cage door stayed open. The Lydon family believes in freedom.

"Some parents are too quick to condemn their children. After my own mum stopped me having a dancing career, I swore I'd even allow my kids to become roadsweepers if that's what made them happy.

"Life's hard enough to-day without pushing your children into something they don't want to do. That's how parents lose their children. Take religion. We're Roman Catholics. Johnnie used to be a churchgoer. If he comes back to it, he'll return on his own. Not because I've pushed him."

And marriage? Despite all the outward rebellion, she believes in marriage — for herself. For Johnny, she's not so sure. "What with all the travelling, it might be better not."

While her son reaches for the stars, Eileen Lydon's feet remain firmly on the ground. For her, the Finsbury Park flat is home.

"Now that Johnny's on the up,' the neighbours say, 'I suppose he'll soon be buying you a grand house in the country.' What they don't understand is that I'm quite happy here.

"And, with all the money in the world, I'd still go to work. Being house-proud, I found myself getting over-fussy and annoying the children. So the answer was to get out of the house."

Johnny Rotten could hardly wish for a better mum. Not only is she his best ally, but she's the Sex Pistols' No 1 fan. "I'd do anything for music. If it wasn't for keeping home, I'd go everywhere with them."

● JOHNNY ROTTEN . . . . not the monster he's made out to be says his mother who lives in a council flat on Finsbury Park's Six Acres Estate.

SEX PISTOLS

'A friend of ours

27 FRI   Virgin Records release the Sex Pistols single 'God Save The Queen'. 50,000 copies are initially pressed. It is banned from receiving Radio One daytime airplay and Woolworths, W.H. Smith's and other national chains refuse to stock the record.

28 SAT   Full page adverts for 'God Save The Queen' appear on the back pages of New Musical Express and Sounds.

EVENTS WHERE EXACT DATE IS UNKNOWN:

The Sex Pistols and the Clash have plans for a two-day punk festival to be held in Bristol. The proposed date is the end of June with the Sex Pistols topping the bill one night and the Clash the other night. Bristol City Council refuse the application.

3 FRI   Sex Pistols single 'God Save The Queen' is reported to have sold 150,000 copies in just five days.

4 SAT   Sounds runs an apology to the Sex Pistols because their advert the previous week had been 'altered from its original form' by the printers.

Sounds includes a full page article from the Islington Gazette of an interview with Johnny Rotten's Mum.

7 TUES   The Sex Pistols Boat Party gets underway at 6.30 in the evening. A boat named 'Queen Elizabeth' is hired by Virgin Records for £500 and sails down the River Thames. When the boat reaches the Houses of Parliament the band launch into 'Anarchy In The UK'. Jah Wobble attacks a French cameraman and this incident makes the captain take the boat back. He radios for the Police. Upon docking the Police appear on the quay. Several people are booked and arrested including: Malcolm, Vivien, Sophie, Alex, Debbie, Tracie, Ben Kelly, Chris Walsh, Jose Esquibel, Jamie Reid and James Lydon. The charges include: Obstruction, assault, threatening behaviour and insulting words likely to cause a breach of the peace. Other songs performed include: 'God Save The Queen'/'Holidays In The Sun'/'Anarchy In The UK' (again)/'Pretty Vacant'/'Problems'.

8 WED   Malcolm McLaren appears at Bow Street Magistrates Court charged with insulting behaviour, following the boat party the previous evening. He pleads not guilty and is released on £100 bail until August 30th. Johnny's brother, James Lydon is fined £3 after he pleads guilty to shouting and swearing on Victoria Embankment.

Sex Pistols sign with Virgin Records for Europe for the sum of £75,000.

DAILY Mirror

BRITAIN'S BIGGEST DAILY SALE 7p   Tuesday, June 21, 1977

SLASHED !

Razor attack on Rotten, the Punk Rocker

JOHNNY ROTTEN, king of punk rock, has had his face slashed in a frenzied razor attack by a gang who ambushed him outside a pub.

The pop world fears the slashing is only the start of a savage backlash against punk rock groups such as the Sex Pistol's, with whom Rotten is lead singer.

The Sex Pistols are believed to be prime targets because of their anti-Royal record "God save the Queen" — an outrageous disc banned by the BBC — that condemn the Queen as a moron.

The attack on Rotten — whose real name is John Lydon — was the second on the group within days. A Sex Pistols art director was beaten up in the street last week and left with a broken nose and a broken leg.

Marked

Rotten had his face slashed on Saturday night in the car park of the Pegasus pub, near the Wessex Sound Studios in Highbury, London.

Two men with him — recording studios manager Bill Price and record producer Chris Thomas — were both wounded and needed hospital treatment.

Bill Price said last night: "We were probably marked down for attack when Johnny Rotten was recognised in the pub.

"As we left, the gang — about nine men, all in their thirties — bounced, waving razors and knives and aiming for Johnny.

"They cut his face and his arm but didn't manage to do any serious damage.

"Chris also got his face cut by a knife or razor and I got a deep cut in my arm trying to fend off the blows.

It was obvious Johnny was the target. He's not too popular

By STUART GREIG

because of the record about the Queen.

"We were lucky to get away in one piece.

The attackers seemed to be out to mark us rather than kill us."

A spokesman for Virgin Records said: "It looks like punk rockers are in for a hard time.

"A lot of people were upset about the record about the Queen and that could be part of the problem.

"Johnny is a target because he is the king of the punk rockers — the figurehead.

But he is non-violent and we're going to have to take special care to protect him"

A Scotland Yard spokesman said last night: "We are investigating this unprovoked attack."

JOHNNY ROTTEN . . . a backlash victim — with more to come?

Continuing saga of the Pistols v. Establishment

THE SEX PISTOLS continued to face hassles from the Establishment when a Jubilee boat trip they had organised last Tuesday was brought to a premature close after the police moved in.

Ten people, including the Pistols' manager, Malcolm MacLaren, were arrested and charged with various offences including obstructing the police, unlawful obstruction, threatening behaviour, being drunk and disorderly, using insulting words and assault.

All ten people pleaded not guilty at Bow Street magistrates court and were remanded on bail.

Around 200 people had been on the boat, called 'Queen Elizabeth', and the Sex Pistols played a set, which was halted when the power supply was cut off. The boat was 'buzzed' by police boats and returned to the shore. The arrest occurred when the police tried to move the voyagers off the boat.

For a report on the Jubilee boat see page nine.

Meanwhile, the Pistols' single, 'God Save The Queen' climbed to number two in the singles charts, despite being banned by all BBC and independent television and radio stations.

There is little doubt that it was the fastest selling single last week but the fact that several of the 'chart return' shops had banned the single kept it from the number one spot.

Virgin Records said this week that the record was maintaining its sales figures. A spokesperson said: "If it does get to number one then it will prove that the much-vaunted power of radio and television is negligible if the public interest is already there."

And London is now virtually a closed city for the Pistols as far as live gigs are concerned. A planned concert at the Rainbow Theatre had to be abandoned after the theatre's own insurance company refused to cover the concert and the GLC raised objection.

And even outside the capital the situation is much the same. Malcolm MacLaren is told SOUNDS this week that "it is impossible for us to put a structured tour together at the moment".

However MacLaren was hopeful that something would be sorted out and there is still a possibility of an outdoor punk festival featuring the Pistols in the West Country.

And this week came news that a group of MPs, including Marcus Lipton Labour MP for Lambeth Central and Neville Trotter Tory member for Tynemouth, are trying to get the Pistols' single banned.

They were joined by DJ Tony Blackburn who said of the record: "It is disgraceful and makes me ashamed of the pop world but it is a fad that won't last."

A spokesperson for Virgin replied: "It is remarkable that MPs should have nothing better to do than get agitated about records which were never intended for their tiny minds or sensibilities.

"As for Tony Blackburn he makes us all ashamed. But he is a fad that won't last." In fact, the record was broadcast last saturday on Radio London by Charlie Gillett on his Honky Tonk programme — complained.

10 FRI   Sex Pistols single 'God Save The Queen' has sold 200,000 copies in the first two weeks of release.

11 SAT   Record Mirror has a colour photo of the Sex Pistols on its cover and a two page interview inside.

13 MON   Jamie Reid (art designer) is attacked by a gang of 4 youths and receives a broken nose and a cracked bone in his leg.

17 FRI   'God Save The Queen' by the Sex Pistols reaches No 2 in the national charts. It almost certainly was No 1 but the people who compile the charts (British Market Research Bureau) probably find some 'legal' way to announce it as only reaching No 2. CBS who manufacture both the Sex Pistols and Rod Stewart who is said to be No. 1 confirm that God Save The Queen has sold more!

18 SAT   Johnny Rotten, producer Chris Thomas and engineer Bill Price are attacked with razors by a gang as they leave the Pegasus pub in Highbury, North London while taking a break from recording in nearby Wessex studio. John is taken to Hospital and is given two stitches in his arm.

New Musical Express includes an 'Eye Witness' account of the Sex Pistols Boat Party.

19 SUN   Paul Cook is attacked by five men yielding knives and an iron bar outside Shepherds Bush tube station. He is taken to Hospital and receives 15 stitches to the back of his head.

21 TUES   It is decided that 'Pretty Vacant' with B side 'No Fun' will be the next single.

23 THUR   A second attack on Johnny Rotten takes place. This time at Dingwalls Dance Hall in Camden.

25 SAT   Sounds back page has an advert for the Sex Pistols single 'God Save The Queen' showing all the radio stations, shops, etc. that have banned the record.

27 MON   Concerts in Scandinavia are set up for July.

EVENTS WHERE EXACT DATE IS UNKNOWN:

The Sex Pistols 30 second radio advert consisting of the juxtaposition of the national anthem and their single 'God Save The Queen' is refused by BRMB, Piccadilly, Clyde and Capital. A more conventional version using only the single is later accepted.

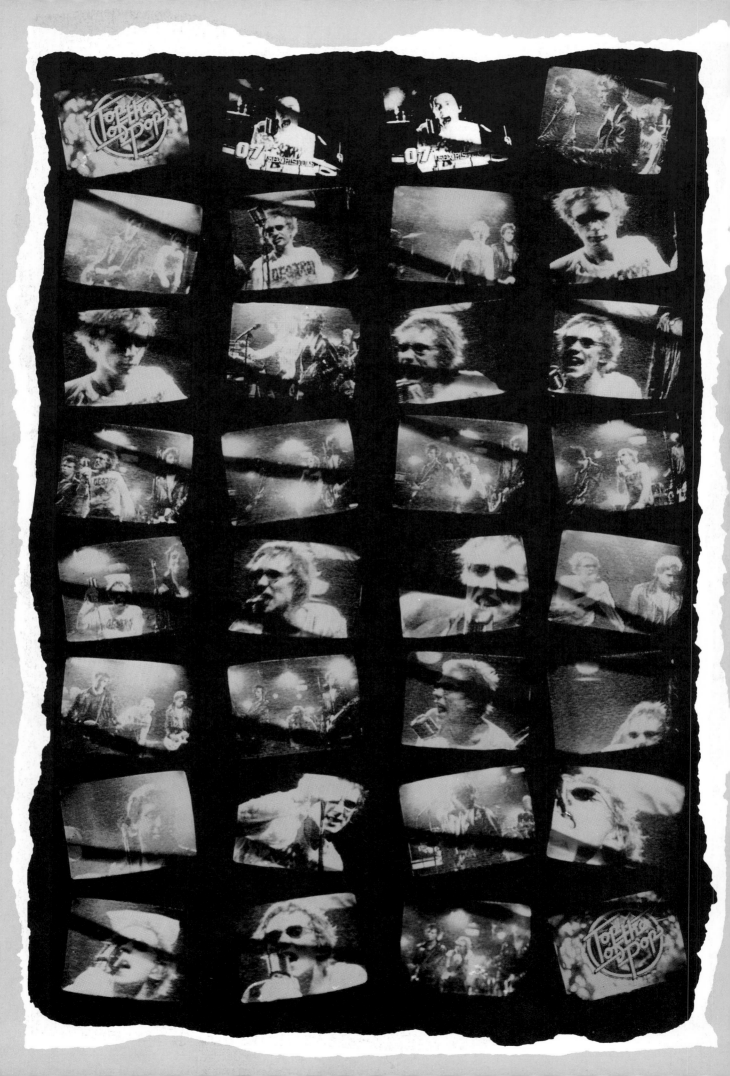

2 SAT   'Pretty Vacant' is released on Virgin Records.

3 SUN   Malcolm McLaren flies to Los Angeles to meet Russ Meyer and start work on the proposed Sex Pistols film.

5 TUES   Filming of the promo video for 'Pretty Vacant' takes place.

7 THUR   Nancy Spungen (girlfriend of Sid Vicious) appears in court for carrying a truncheon in her handbag "for protection". She is saved from being sent home to the USA after the court hears that Sid Vicious is intending to marry her!

11 MON   Johnny Rotten records a radio programme with Tommy Vance to be broadcast on Capital Radio on July 16th under the banner "The Punk and his Music".

13 WED   Malcolm phones from Los Angeles to tell Virgin that the video of 'Pretty Vacant' should not be offered to Top of the Pops TV show. Richard Branson says that they "can't get the film back off TOTP".

Sex Pistols fly out from England at 10.40 am to play Copenhagen in Denmark, Daddy's Dance Hall. This is the first night of a two week Scandinavian tour. The road crew includes Rodent (borrowed from the Clash) and Boogie. Songs performed: 'Anarchy In The UK'/'I Wanna Be Me'/'Seventeen'/'New York'/'Satellite'/'No Feelings'/'No Fun'/'Holidays In The Sun'/'Problems'/'Pretty Vacant'/'God Save The Queen' (**).

14 THUR   Sex Pistols play Copenhagen, Daddy's Dance Hall (2nd night) songs performed: 'Anarchy In The UK'/'I Wanna Be Me'/ 'Seventeen'/'New York'/'EMI'/'No Feelings'/'Pretty Vacant'/'Problems'/ 'God Save The Queen'/'No Fun' (**).

Video of 'Pretty Vacant' is shown on 'Top of the Pops' TV show. The single is number 7 in the charts!

15 FRI   Halmstad, Sweden, Beach Disco. Songs performed: 'Anarchy In The UK'/'I Wanna Be Me'/'Seventeen'/'New York'/'EMI'/'No Feelings'/'Pretty Vacant'/'Problems'/'God Save The Queen' (**).

Glitterbest move offices to Shaftesbury Avenue in London.

16 SAT   Helsingborg, Mogambo Disco. Songs performed: 'Anarchy In The UK'/'I Wanna Be Me'/'Seventeen'/'New York'/'EMI'/'Problems'/ 'No Feelings'/'Pretty Vacant'/'God Save The Queen' (**) possibly this show (or part of it) is broadcast on Swedish radio?

The pre-recorded (11th) hour long interview between Johnny Rotten and Tommy Vance is broadcast on London's Capital Radio.

17 SUN   Sex Pistols play Jonkoping in Sweden, Disco 42.

18 MON   Day spent travelling to next gig.

LET HIM WHO IS WITHOUT SID . . .

Vicious in Court Drama

Bekantas bekanta

"ETT DJÄVLA STÄLLE", tyckte Sex Pistols om Köpenhamn

ON TUESDAY morning at Wells Street Magistrates' Court, a Teddy Boy had just been sent off with a stiff fine for partaking in a bit of punk-bashing down Kings Road and being caught with an offensive weapon, when he sauntered out of the courtroom at 10.30 am to be faced by no less than four punks waiting in the hall, all looking suitably mean.

Was this Karma? He might well have thought at the time. Well, it wasn't — in fact the scrawniest and most evil-looking one was being had up on exactly the same charge as him.

His name was Sid Vicious, and he'd flown straight in from the Sex Pistols' Scandanavian tour to stand trial on a year-old charge of being caught in Oxford Street's 100 Club with a flick-knife the night a 17-year-old girl had one eye blinded by a piece of flying glass. Standing with him as a witness for the defence were Clash members Mick Jones and Paul Simenon, plus journalist Caroline Coon and ex-journalist/Generation X manager John Ingham.

On the prosecution side was merely one policeman, and no civilian witnesses whatsoever. In fact, to the impartial observer the whole scam appeared as something of a put-up job, and one reason for the trial being postponed until virtually a year after the event was said to be that the police involved had such an insubstantial case.

Anyway, Vicious himself wasn't taking any chances. He'd even bought a black suit and donned a shirt and tie

for the occasion. Only a pair of fairly brutal 'beetle crushers' with thick rubber soles gave his identity away. He'd even dragged his mother along, exhumed from darkest Dalston for the day on her 250cc motorbike, which was parked outside the West End assizes.

Meanwhile, Messrs Simenon and Jones appeared to be in a fairly dire state, having spent the previous evening getting outrageously pissed at the CBS Convention and refusing to be photographed with Chairman Oberstein. Anyway, each witness spent between twenty and thirty minutes in the box and the basic insubstantial nature of the charges became apparent.

All witnesses for the defence claimed that Vicious was over at the opposite side of the 100 Club when the fatal glass was thrown, though that wasn't even the charge, of course.

Apparently, no less than five policemen were called to the club and Vicious, who'd made something of a name for himself previously for various outbursts of violence at punk gigs, was immediately selected, quite indiscriminately, as the potential culprit. The Five Feds pounced, dragging Vicious out of the club and searching him to find a flick-knife.

The outcome of all this hoo-hah was that the presiding judge, a conservative type (Get away — Ed) with a fairly obvious bias against punks (You don't say — Ed), gave Vicious a stern reprimand and a fine of £125 after his lawyer had given a speech about the possibility of this upstanding young man's future in the Sex Pistols combo being jinxed by a stiff sentence.

After the trial, Sid flew back to Scandinavia to play the remaining dates with his band and socialise with Charles Shaar Murray.

□ NICK KENT

Now turn to page 23.

SYDSVENSKA DAGBLADET SNÄLLPOSTEN Fredagen den 15 juli 1977

— Vi vågar inte gå ut i London

Punkare hit i "landsflykt"

Försök till förbud

19 TUES   Kristinehamn in Sweden, Club Zebra.

20 WED   Oslo in Norway, at 7.30 the band attend a press conference
             and later play at the Pingvinen Restaurant. Songs performed:
'Anarchy In The UK'/'I Wanna Be Me'/'Seventeen'/'New York'/'EMI'/'No
Fun'/'No Feelings'/'Problems'/'Pretty Vacant'/'God Save The Queen' (**).

Birthday of Paul Cook of the Sex Pistols born this day 1956.

21 THUR   Trondheim in Norway, Student Ssamfundet club.

The video of 'Pretty Vacant' is shown on Top Of The Pops TV show?

22 FRI   The French issue of 'Anarchy In The UK' on Glitterbest/
             Barclay Records is being imported into the UK.

23 SAT   Vaxjo, Sweden. Barbarella's (They play here for two nights).
             Opening song is 'Anarchy In The UK', the 3rd song is
'Seventeen' then 'EMI', 'No Fun' and the last song is 'God Save The
Queen' which at that time was number 8 in the Swedish charts. 'Pretty
Vacant' is played as an encore. Tonight's concert is for 15 to 20 year
olds only.

24 SUN   Barbarella's, Vaxjo, Sweden (2nd night for over 21's only).
             opening song is 'Anarchy In The UK', they also play 'Liar'
and 'Submission' both of which they didn't play the previous night. The
encore is 'No Fun'.

25 MON   Sid Vicious makes a flying visit to England in the middle of
             the Sex Pistols Scandinavian tour to appear in court (26th)
on a charge of being caught at the 100 club with a flick knife on the
2nd night of the legendary 'Punk Festival' in September last year. Sid
wears a black suit with shirt and tie. He is fined £125.

27 WED   Stockholm, Student Karen, Happy House. Admission to over 23's
             only! Songs performed: 'Anarchy In The UK'/'I Wanna Be Me'/
'Seventeen'/'New York'/'EMI'/'God Save The Queen'/'Problems'/'No Feel-
ings'/'Pretty Vacant'/'No Fun'. (possibly they also played 'Liar' and
'Submission')?

28 THUR   Stockholm, Student Karen, Happy House (2nd night) This is for
             15 year olds and over. Songs performed: 'Anarchy In The UK'
/'I Wanna Be Me'/'Seventeen'/'New York'/'EMI'/'Submission'/'No Feelings'
/'Problems'/'God Save The Queen'/'Pretty Vacant'/'No Fun' (**). All
tracks (except 'No Feelings' and 'No Fun') issued on the bootleg record
called Bad Boys, taken from a Swedish radio broadcast.

29 FRI   Linkoping in Sweden. The last day of their tour. Malcolm flies
             back from Los Angeles.

30 SAT   Sex Pistols fly back to the UK from Sweden and return to
             Wessex recording studio.

Melody Maker

AUGUST 20, 1977   **15p weekly**   **USA 75 cents**

PISTOLS ROLLING ANARCHY REVUE

JOHNNY ROTTEN/STEVE HILLAGE

THE SEX PISTOLS, for many months musical outcasts in their own country, are about to set out on a "guerrilla" tour of Britain, playing about 20 dates under assumed names. The tour will start later this month and carry on through October, with the band arriving unannounced at a venue, leaving only a few hours for word to spread on the local grapevine.

If word gets out before the day of the concert and the details are published, the concert will be scrapped.

The band's agency, Cowbell, has strenuously denied that the tour is taking place, but MM understands that about 20 dates have been arranged, with concerts in Birmingham and Swindon at least.

The band have been deliberately booked into low-key venues, mainly independent clubs off the big circuits. The aim is that word-of-mouth will avoid the vast crowds and possible trouble that advance publicity would bring.

This will be the first time the Pistols have played regular concerts in Britain for about ten months. After finishing the recording of their debut album, which is due out on Virgin at the end of September, they were forced by controversy to tour in Scandinavia.

Club Lafayette PRESENTS MYSTERY GROUP WHO WILL BE KNOWN AS **THE SPOTS**

FRIDAY 19th AUGUST ADMISSION £1

MEMBERS COMPS NOT VALID THIS NIGHT

Ain't Bin To No Music Scho

Their new single on Rabid Records

Club Lafayette PRESENTS MYSTERY GROUP WHO WILL BE

THE Roxy Club
41/43 NEAL ST., COVENT GARDEN, WC2

Wednesday 17th August
Audition Night. Adm 50p
DOLE QUEUE RABIES & COOL THRUST

Thursday 18th August
LONDON JOHNNY CURIOUS & STRANGERS

Friday 19th August
EATER THE DEAD

Saturday 20th August
SHAM 69 MENACE

THE Roxy Club
41/43 NEAL ST., COVENT GARDEN, WC2

Tuesday, August 23rd
Audition Night. Adm. 50p
SPEEDOMETERS Crabs Tax Exiles

Wednesday, August 24th
Audition Night. Adm. 50p
PINK PARTS Stormtroopers

Thursday, August 25th
SLAUGHTER & THE DOGS + Varicose Veins

Friday, August 26th
WASPS + Rabies

Saturday, August 27th

4 THUR Steve Jones and Paul Cook jam with the Only Ones when they play the Speakeasy in London.

5 FRI/
6 SAT The 2nd European Punk Festival at Mont de Marsan in France includes: 5th: The Damned, the Boys, the Rich Kids, the Police, Wayne County & the Electric Chairs, and Asphalt Jungle. 6th: Eddie & the Hot Rods, Dr. Feelgood, Tyla Gang, Little Bob Story, the Jam, the Rings, Bijou and Marie a Legarson.

7 SUN London Weekend Television re-screen Janet Street Porter's Sex Pistols interview, originally broadcast before the infamous Bill Grundy show last year.

8 MON Russ Meyer arrives in London for talks on the proposed Sex Pistols film.

17 WED When copies of Melody Maker (dated 20th) hit the streets they includes a front page story with details of the Pistols 'secret tour'. However, the details are very patchy.

19 FRI Sex Pistols begin their 'undercover' UK tour when they play a 'Secret gig' at Wolverhampton, Lafayette Club under the name of the "Spots" which stands for: 'Sex Pistols On Tour Secretly'. Songs performed: 'Anarchy In The UK'/'I Wanna Be Me'/'Seventeen'/'New York'/'EMI'/'Holidays In The Sun'/'No Feelings'/'Problems'/'Pretty Vacant'/'God Save The Queen' plus 'No Fun' as encore. They are supposedly paid £50 for the performance! Admission price charged by the club is £1.50 even though the posters state £1.00.

20 SAT Melody Maker includes a 'review' of a Sex Pistols bootleg album titled 'The Good Time Music of the Sex Pistols' which they say was recorded at the Lesser Free Trade Hall in Manchester in June 1976. They also reveal rumours of two more albums – Burton '76 which did come out under the banner 'Indecent Exposure' and 'Bogarts' which was never issued.

22 MON The final draft of the planned film 'God Save The Queen' is finished.

23 TUES The Roxy Club in London holds its 'Audition Night' and includes in its advertising a band called the 'Tax Exiles'. The following night (24th) in Doncaster, the Sex Pistols play under the name 'the Tax Exiles'. Malcolm was planning for the Sex Pistols to play the Roxy Club but it never happened and even the band never knew!

24 WED The Sex Pistols play Doncaster, Outlook Club under the name of 'The Tax Exiles'. Songs performed: 'Anarchy In The UK'/'I Wanna Be Me'/'Seventeen'/'New York'/'EMI'/'Holidays In The Sun'/'No Feelings'/'Problems'/'Pretty Vacant'/'God Save The Queen'/'No Fun' (**).

Sid Vicious finds a flat in Maida Vale with a 7 year lease (running to 1984) Malcolm McLaren is heard to say "That's OK, He'll be dead by then". Billy Idol later takes over the flat before moving to New York.

Back with a bullet

Meet the Rich Kids, featuring Glen Matlock, co-writer of 'Anarchy In The UK', 'God Save The Queen' and 'Pretty Vacant'

Interview by PETE SILVERTON

GLEN MATLOCK/STEVE NEW: 'The Pistols was good practice'

Pix by IAN DICKSON

COMING DOWN from the Harrow Road by bus, Steve New's getting the rise taken out of him by a bunch of kids because he's wearing carpet slippers ("It was pouring and me 'boots have got holes in 'em and I didn't want to get me feet wet"). The bravest of the kids comes over and screams into Steve's ear: "And we don't *caaarre . . .*!" That poor malchick just didn't understand the irony of his words.

Steve, y'see, plays guitar for the Rich Kids, a rock 'n' roll band. And the Rich Kids' bassist is a personable geezer, name of Glen Matlock. And, in case you didn't know or your memory's really that short or just hated punk back then, Glen used to be in a band called the Sex Pistols. He was with them till just fourfore they signed that short lived contract with A&M. He played on 'Anarchy'. In fact, he wrote the tune. And he wrote the tune for 'God Save The Queen'. And he wrote 'Pretty Vacant'. All of it.

"John (Rotten, singer) did change two faces. So he can say it's his. He did come up with two good ones though.

Surprisingly, there's not a trace of bitterness in Glen's voice when he tells me that. Just lounging back on the sofa in his flat, just a hefty gob from the Arsenal ground. There's no need for such acrimony.

Firstly, as you'll see later, he's well pleased to be shot of some of the scenes around the Pistols and Malcolm McLaren. Secondly, in the Rich Kids, he's got his own world-beater of a band.

I'VE KNOWN Glen pretty well for eighteen months or so now and when he told me just after leaving the Pistols that he was getting a new band together, they were gonna be great and I'd better believe it. I did.

But, when I did eventually get to see them play, even I was surprised how good they were. A word of mouth only (even those supposedly "in the know" didn't this time round gig supporting the Tom Robinson band on a free night at the Brecknock is hardly a star-blazing start but that's

how Glen wanted it and the quality of the band still shone through like a galactic explosion.

I can only think of one other new band this year who've impressed me so much first time of seeing, the Radiators from Space, and even they were still in a formative, tentative, unpolished stage of their evolution.

Mind you, anyone expecting Glen to be taking up where he left the Pistols is in for a shock. There's none of the Pistols' obvious affinities with heavy metal. The Rich Kids are pop, albeit heavy pop. Taut, emphatic little songs with crafty lyrics (but you'd know that already after hearing 'Pretty Vacant'). Drums, bass, two guitar spellbind dynamism personified.

A year on, there's endless Pistols copyists. Six months on, there's endless Clash copyists. In six months time, there's gonna be the same number of Rich Kids copyists.

If, that is, they can get one rather large problem sorted out. The Kids are still one member short of perfection. They've yet to find a fourth member, the singer/guitarist/dancer of their dreams.

"We know exactly who we want. We call him Jimmy Norton" Which is why at the Brecknock (and the night before at the Vortex) they temporarily borrowed the main contender for the vacant-waste looking-man alive crown, Mick Jones. Only *borrowed*, notice. Before any of you get hold of the wrong end of the guitar neck, let me tell you that Mick has not, repeat not, left the Clash to join the Rich Kids. He was just helping them out. That's all.

MICK JONES/GLEN/STEVE NEW: "We do a better version of 'Pretty Vacant'."

Glen: "Mick's an old mate. When he was getting the Clash together, I used to play bass for him to audition drummers. Now he's doing the same for me. Except we're actually playing gigs. He's great. I've always wanted to play with Mick. And now I have. We were getting pissed the other night and I asked him to do it and he said okay. It's as simple as that."

So, if you saw either of the gigs, you have a right to feel a little bit smug (even if you didn't know it) 'cos you were blessed with the rare privilege of eyeballing the Matlock/Jones All

Stars. If you didn't . . . tough luck. 'Cos there ain't gonna be any more. This is what you want to know.

The Eight songs. 'Burning Sounds'. The eponymous 'Rich Kids'. The old Pistols/Matlock chestnut, 'No Lip' ('Pushin' and Shovin'). The cross-current riffing of '(I Ain't) Too Alone Now'. 'Strange One'. 'Empty Words (Are All I Hear)' (Steve: "It's about talking loud and saying nothing"). And finally the very well-known 'Pretty Vacant' which surprised the section of the audience who only recognised Mick Jones until they were firmly told that this wasn't some lame cover-version but the real original. But if they had ears they realised that anyway.

Glen: "Nah, I don't mind the Pistols doing it. 'Cos we do a better version. They really cocked it up."

Glen even committed the ultimate crime (for a punk band) of then introducing the members of the band while they choogled along behind him.

"Thanks to Mick Jones for coming along." Mick goosey-ganders (Glen's phrase) forward, arms everywhichway, knees knocking in some kind of frenzied idiosyncratic

frug and blasts out his solo.

"Thanks to Steve New. He's an intimate part of the female anatomy." Steve obliges by ripping out a few notes from his big-bodied country-looking rock 'n' roll sounding guitar. He's almost as good a foil for Mick Jones' playing as Mr. Strummer.

And last but not least (just tucked away at the back), the one with the bleeding hands, Rusty Egan, the drummer. He's what an earlier generation would have called a wide boy. He's the bloke with the proverbial more front than Selfridges. He's got as much mouth as a junior Muhammed Ali and the cheerful nous of a market trader.

He's been with the Kids since just after Glen left the Nashville. "I met Rusty down the Nashville. I didn't know who he was but he is a bit of a mouth and he convinced me he should be me drummer. He's such a con man that he'd been me drummer for two weeks before I heard him play. Would you buy a used drumkit from this man?"

No, but I could listen to him play one all night (as long as he doesn't

continues page 12

RICH KIDS (Matlock on right) jam with Tom Robinson Band and Clash's Mick Jones

from page 10

solo anyhow).

Steve, who'd been in the Pistols for a couple of months two years ago joined just after Rusty and the three of them have been trading under the name the Rich Kids ever since. And looking for that elusive fourth member. They came closest with Midge Ure from Slik.

"Midge was gonna join the Pistols at the time. Malcom (McLaren) and Bernie (Rhodes, Clash manager) went up north to sell some gear and Midge bought an amp off 'em and they told him about the band. When they got back to London they called him up but he said: 'No, I've got this band called Slik now'.

"And then we got John for the Pistols and Midge was on Top of the Pops. But I always reckoned him as a rocker. So after leaving the Pistols I gave him a call and he came down and he was great. We did a few gigs (also unannounced) together but it didn't work out. He's just a kind of Scotman. I understood really 'cos it

meant doing it on our terms giving everything up and moving down to London.

NOW YOU know the Rich Kids story up-to-date, although you won't have a chance to hear how good they are in person until they find that fourth man. But what of Glen's earlier days with the Festival of Light's favourite band? The split wasn't very amicable to say the least, was it?

"Look, you know it had been building up for a long time. You saw me on the Anarchy tour up in Manchester and you saw what it was like within the band (actually I didn't really because I was more pre-occupied with Joe Strummer wanting to stick one on me). There was so much bitchiness in the Pistols camp about the other bands on the tour. Now they've come out and said it all in the open which is alright but all that stuff behind the back was just . . childish."

How long had it been building up?

"There was always a crisis situation in that band. John'd leave. Steve'd leave. Paul'd leave. I'd left twice before. Third time lucky.

"What people don't always understand is that I'd been in the Pistols (though they weren't always called that) since I was 16. I'm 21 now. So it's not exactly an overnight success.

"I went to the grammar school and Steve and Paul went to the local comprehensive but I knew 'em from playing football against them. When we started we used to dress like a mod band. We all went out and bought Hush Puppies and played Small Faces numbers. But we knew at the back of it we had this great idea. Nobody sat down an' thought about it but we all knew what was needed. I wanted to be in a band 'cos I'd never seen the band I liked.

"Me, Steve and Paul were all a bit into the Faces but we thought that Rod Stewart was just a prick. So we had that rock 'n' roll side of it. Ideas-wise we realised it had to be something else and when we met John he sort of encapsulated it."

How much difference did John make?

"It was complete then. We'd had the music but he had the words. He was the guy with the actual gab. We saw that the day we met him. That day I wrote 'Pretty Vacant' (this is two years ago). I'd seen this poster for Television in Malcolm's shop. It had all these great song titles like 'The Arms of Venus de Milo' and 'Love Comes in Spurts'. And it just came to me. I wrote 'Pretty Vacant' on the train going home.

"And we all know what's happened since then. But what about Malcom?

"I just needed a Saturday job (while he was at school and, later, St. Martin's Art School) and walked into Malcom's shop." (Back when it was called 'Let it Rock' and specialised in fifties nostalgia gear.)

How well did you get on with Malcom?

"Not much. I was working for him in the shop and I was working for him at the end. That's one of the reasons I split. It had been four years and it hadn't changed. He just doesn't give you any respect for what you're doing."

What about the accusations of the Pistols being his puppets?

"He certainly pulls the strings. Now more than ever. They need him. It's him who told them not to play any gigs in Britain. I ask you, who's building images or who's building images? But unless you've got a little bit of suss about you, you don't realise he's doing it.

"No Fun's' a horror of a record. We were only taking the piss when we did it. We were doing a hippy version. But Malcom loved it so it's gotta go out.

"It really got to me towards the end. When we were in Amsterdam, I'd just woken up and someone handed me the phone and told me it was the Daily Mirror. This bloke says 'You've been sacked by EMI. What do you think of that?'' I said "Well, it's a laugh." and I really got slated by Malcom for that. But it was a laugh.

Two minutes on the label and you get the sack. It's got to be a laugh.

"All those sort of little things. When you can't say what you want to say, it's time for something else. When the band becomes more important than the people involved, it's just like doing a job, sitting at a desk and that's what I'm in rock 'n' roll to avoid."

What about that remark when you left — "He liked the Beatles so we got rid of him"?

"They had to appear in complete control even when they weren't, didn't they? And what kind of reason is that for getting a guy out of a band? I hate the Beatles for the same reason as they did but anybody who doesn't admit the Beatles were great is dopey and if you feel that threatened by a band that broke up seven years ago. . ."

Ever see 'em these days?

"Nah, I don't go down the Speakeasy very often."

Any regrets?

"Nah. The idea (of the Pistols) was so great. There was no question about it. I didn't have to worry about where the next meal was coming from although I didn't have one at the time. We all knew we were going to be famous. And the Pistols was great practice. You had to really fight to get your ideas through. It took me three weeks to get them round to my way of doing 'God Save The Queen'. But they came round. It made it seem easy with these guys (pointing to Steve)."

Which brings us back to the present and the Rich Kids.

You might not have to rely on my word for their greatness for too long because there's a strong possibility of their putting out a single as a trio. But they can't play live again till they find that fourth member. They (and you and I) need him desperately. How close do you think he is, Glen?

"As close as walking round the corner and bumping into him."

Whoever you are, bump into Glen quick, huh?

25 THUR   Sex Pistols play Scarborough under the name 'Special Guest'.
            Bury St. Edmunds had been planned for this date under the
            name of 'The Hampsters' but was never played.

26 FRI   Sex Pistols play Middlesborough, Rock Garden under the name
            of 'Acne Rabble'. Songs played include 'Anarchy In The
UK'/'I Wanna Be Me'/'Seventeen'/'New York'/'EMI'/'Holidays In The Sun'/
'No Feelings'/'Problems'/'Pretty Vacant'/'God Save The Queen' plus an
encore of 'No Fun'.

27 SAT   Birthday of Glen Matlock born this day 1956.

28 SUN   A concert was planned for Manchester but was never played.

30 TUES   Sex Pistols in the recording studio.

31 WED   Sex Pistols play Plymouth, Woods Centre as 'The Hampsters'.

EVENTS WHERE EXACT DATE IS UNKNOWN:

Sex Pistols attempt to play Bristol, The Granary under the name of 'The
    Hampsters' but the word leaks out too quickly and they decide
    against it.

 1 THUR   Sex Pistols play Penzance, Winter Gardens where they are
            advertised as "A mystery band of international repute". About
400 people turn up. Songs performed include 'Anarchy In The UK'/'I
Wanna Be Me'/'God Save The Queen'/'Seventeen'/'Holidays In The Sun'/
'EMI'/'No Feelings' plus an encore of 'No Fun' and 'Anarchy In The
UK'. The gig is filmed and recorded, probably by Julian Temple. This is
almost certainly the final night of the so-called 'SPOTS' tour.

 3 SAT   Birthday of Steve Jones of the Sex Pistols born this day 1955.

A pre-recorded interview with the Sex Pistols is broadcast on BBC Radio
Cleveland.

Sounds includes a feature on Glen Matlock's new band, The Rich Kids.

13 TUES   Debbie Wilson is acquitted while Sophie Richmond is fined £10
            for obstructing a police officer at the Sex Pistols Jubilee boat
trip earlier in the year (June 7th).

*"Wanna destroy passers by
'Cause I wanna be—
Anarchy! . . ."*

*"I dedicate to you
All my love
My whole life thru —
I love you
Forever and ever . . ."*

BLACKMAIL CORNER SPECIAL

IAN CRANNA sees the dying gasps of SLIK, former teenybop idols-for-a-day — and talks to MIDGE URE about the time he nearly became a SEX PISTOL.

THE MAN WHO WAS ALMOST ROTTEN

FORMER SEX PISTOLS bassist Glen Matlock is expected to announce the completion of his new Rich Kids band later this week.

With the almost certain addition of ex-Slik vocalist/guitarist Midge Ure, it will be the culmination of an association between Matlock and Ure which began over two years ago — when Midge Ure was originally considered as The Sex Pistols' lead singer.

It has now come to light that shortly before Ure's ascendance to teenybop idolhood, he was asked to join the Pistols by Malcolm McLaren and his then sidekick Bernard Rhodes (now, of course, manager of The Clash).

Ure, however, had his own gig to do.

Thrills spoke to Midge recently at Edinburgh's Tiffany's — venue for one of Slik's last gigs. He explained how he came to be breaking up the band to go join Matlock in London... *and* gave us the details of McLaren's initial invitation to him to join the Pistols.

The gig itself was a revelation.

Despite dismal reaction from a small, unsympathetic crowd, it was a performance of quite stunning power, a magnificent display of blistering high energy rock'n'roll that had your *Thrills*person reaching for the Gig Of The Year hyperboles.

It was a truly extraordinary turn of events for the erstwhile doyens of the screaming teeny hordes. The one compensation is the knowledge that you can find this *real* latterday Slik captured on a triple A-side single under the name of PVC2, on Zoom Records — Scotland's latest independent label. The record to ask for is "Put You In The Picture".

After the gig, *Thrills* cornered Slik in the shoebox dressing room to try to find why on earth they were breaking up such a superb band.

The short answer: they just couldn't lose the teenybop stigma.

"We've been lying low for six months, trying to get a recording contract," says keyboards player Billy McIsaac (hot faces at Arista when Ure joins Rich Kids after that label

chucked him on the scrap-heap, huh?). "But it takes so long for people to forget."

As for the teenies themselves: "They're interested in Flintlock and Donna Summer now," volunteers newish bassist Russell Webb.

And if Slik changed their name?

"What's the point?" shrugs Midge. "You'd still get snide people coming and saying: 'They're still Slik — what the hell are they trying to do?' People are very sadistic, you know.

"It doesn't matter how good you are — it's actually got to the point where if you're not new, or if you've done what we've done — forget it! You've had it."

Midge accurately sketches the grisly fate that would have befallen them had they tried their luck by moving to London: the bedraggled coterie of under-age fans yelling for "Forever And Ever", the half-empty halls, and, if they'd tried a new name, the sneers and disdain that would have greeted them at the Marque of the Vortex.

Ure reckons that several record companies they've hustled since the Arista deal fell through would have grabbed them eagerly — "We've got another Stranglers here!" — *if they weren't Slik.*

Finally it became obvious that one

of them had to leave so that the others could legitimately change their name and kiss off the old image.

"It took the Rich Kids offer for everyone to realise it was the best thing to do," explains Midge. "They were an unknown band with loads and loads of potential — and record companies throwing figures the size of telephone numbers for deals . . . really ridiculous!

"They aren't even as good as Slik musically — and I've told them that as well. And they're getting offered all this . . ."

So Midge decided to vacate the band. Slik will be regrouping with another local hot property, Willie Gardner of Hot Valves. They can't wait to get started.

But what's Midge's version of the Rich Kids saga?

"My version is the real version. The true, unadulterated version!

"I was walking out a music shop in Glasgow two years ago," he begins, "when I was stopped by The Clash's manager — he wasn't their manager then — Bernie Rhodes.

"And he asked me if I played in a band — though I'd no guitar case or anything!"

Uh, this begins to sound familiar. You didn't by any chance have to mime in front of a juke box, did you?

"He asked me if I'd go round and speak to the guy round the corner, in the car. I went round and saw him — it was Malcolm McLaren.

"And he said he was forming this new band — he used to manage The New York Dolls — and he was looking for a singer/guitarist, whatever . . . a few members, anyway, and he tried to talk me into joining them."

Midge was not too impressed with the dynamic duo's other mission in Glasgow either — unfortunately we can't go into it here — and anyway . . . "We'd just done the Martin-Coulter thing, just signed with them, so I told

him I wasn't interested.

"So they went back to London. And I think it was Glen — somebody phoned me, anyway, a couple of days later, to see if I'd changed my mind. But I wasn't interested. At that point I told them who I was with — we'd just changed our name from Salvation to Slik. So nothing else happened."

So you never met any of the Pistols themselves?

"I never met any of the band — just Malcolm McLaren and Bernie Rhodes. That was it."

And how had they heard of you?

"They hadn't! They just stopped me, coming out of a shop — because I *looked* right."

Okay, now let's bring things forward to Rich Kids.

"About three months ago," Midge continues, "Glen got EMI to phone me up and see if I wanted to join behind Slik's back, and I went down to see what it was all about. He came up here too."

Had you seen him between times?

"No. In fact I hadn't a clue what he looked like till I stepped off the train.

"He'd seen me on television, taking me for a rock'n'roller rather than a teenybopper: it had always been in the back of his mind to phone me up some time to see about joining his band.

"I think they tried to get the guy from The Jam, but he'd just signed the Jam deal and he didn't want to do it, obviously. So they've spent all this time looking for someone else."

At first Ure declined Matlock's invitation, but then Slik had a rough couple of months and, as depression settled over the band, he changed his mind. "So I'll go with them now," he adds faintly — and for the first time a low note creeps into the band's high spirits.

This week in London Rich Kids' manager, Gerry Hempstead, declined to confirm that Ure was now definitely in the band with Matlock (bass/vocals), Steve New (guitar) and Rusty Egan (drums) — but it looks 99 per cent certain.

What *Thrills* wants to know is — if Midge Ure *had* joined the Pistols two years ago, would Johnny Rotten have wound up imitating Les McKeown on *Saturday Scene*?

THRILLS

ALTERNATIVE LONDON by Nicholas Saunders — *originally a survival kit for urban hippiedom — was banned amidst much controversy when it first appeared at the tail-end of the last decade.*

The notorious publication has recently been reprinted for the fifth time, and although these days it's lost a few points in the outrage credibility stakes by mellowing out with the passing of time, nevertheless it remains mandatory reading for anyone surviving / thriving in London, just as Ken Walsh's Hitcher's Guide To Europe should never be left out of anyone's back-pack when cruising the continent with a thumb waving.

Alternative London contains information on finding temporary and / or permanent shelter, getting around the city dirt cheap, extensive drug data (from avoiding getting busted through how to roll a spliff to possible fines and prison sentences — shudder!), political community groups and related information, where to go for home-making, a squat, curing VD, getting an abortion, adopting children, getting leaflets / propaganda / whatever published and — how you say — much, much more. It's all about how, when and where, published jointly by the author and Wildwood House, price five pee under two quid — AND WORTH EVERY PEE!!!

File under compulsory purchase, and don't be put off because you never wore an Afghan. If you are, it's strictly your loss, punk.

TONY PARSONS

THRILLS

1 SAT   All the music papers carry advertisments for the Sex Pistols
           new single 'Holidays In The Sun'.

Start of The Johnny Thunders and the Heartbreakers tour at Bristol
Polytechnic where Paul Cook sits in on drums and Steve Jones makes a
'guest appearance' on guitar.

8 SAT   The Sex Pistols film with its new name of 'Who Killed Bambi'
           is finalised.

9 SUN   Paul Cook is arrested for criminal damage on a bus!

15 SAT   'Holidays In The Sun' is released on Virgin records.

20 THUR   'Holidays In The Sun' causes a fuss when the Belgian Travel
           Service issue a summons claiming infringement of copyright of
their summer holiday brochure in regard to the artwork on the record
sleeve. 60,000 sleeves are removed from the offices of Virgin records. The
sleeve is withdrawn from sale. All further copies are sold in a plain
white bag.

28 FRI   Sex Pistols album 'Never Mind The Bollocks' is released with
           advance orders of more than 125,000 and instantly qualifies
for a Gold Disc. Advance information from Virgin records talks of the
possibility of there being two versions of the album. The second version
would be without 'God Save The Queen'. This version could then be sold
in branches of W.H. Smith's, Woolworth's and Boots who have banned the
above track. In the end this idea never happens. Initial copies of the
album come as an eleven track album with a free one-sided single of
'Submission'. Later copies are a more normal twelve track album.

29 SAT   Sounds carries a review of a Sex Pistols bootleg album called
           'Spunk'.

EVENTS WHERE EXACT DATE IS UNKNOWN:

At the end of October Russ Meyer gives up on the proposed Sex Pistols
    film and returns home to the USA.

'TRIAD BOSS'

By ROBERT TRAINI

SCOTLAND YARD have arrested a Chinese restaurant proprietor who is believed to be a top Triad boss.

Detectives are trying to smash two Triads—Chinese secret societies—which are operating in many parts of Britain.

And they described the arrest as a major breakthrough in their fight against protection racketeers, blackmail, heroin-dealing and other crimes.

Arrested

He was taken to — where the John — other Chinese — been held at Harrow — Police Station, Padding — ton, since Monday.

The man was — is off in Newport, Gwe — terday morning.

Sex Pistols film is OFF

THE SEX PISTOLS' much-vaunted debut film "Who Killed Bambi?" is off — at any rate, for the time being. After weeks of preparation, shooting was due to begin at Bray Studios last week — but the project has now been put on the shelf, sets and stages dismantled, and director Russ Meyer has returned to Los Angeles.

The movie was to hav starred Marianne Faithfull, role included a red-hot love with Johnny Rotten!

Reason for the postpone apparently involves finan Initially intended as a low-bu picture, it escalated into £750,000 production, which not the type of film the ba manager Malcolm McLaren or nally planned. It was bei financed by the Michael Whi Organisation, 20th Century Fo Warner Brothers Records an Virgin, but one of these backe (which one is unclear) droppe out — and with the new high budget, it wasn't possible to solve this problem at short notice.

One of the producers, Jeremy Thomas, said he's confident the film will be resurrected in due course — but it was too early to suggest when it might resume.

AND THE SAME TO YOU!

Sex Pistols shoot down 'Colonel Bogey' protest

NEVER MIND THE BOLLOCKS HERE'S THE

THE EIGHT - LETTER word immortalised by troops as they marched to the tune of Colonel Bogey is not indecent, magistrates reluctantly decided yesterday.

That gives punk rocker Johnny Rotten and his foul - mouthed Sex Pistols the chance to put up two fingers to the world and say: "And the same to you!"

And it means that thousands of record sleeves with the word

NEVER MIND . . . Christopher Seale yesterday with the controversial record cover

By BRIAN DIXON

on them can go on display.

Record shop manager Christopher Seale was cleared of four charges, under an 88-year-old law, of displaying indecent printed matter in his store in King Street, Nottingham.

VULGAR

Magistrates at Nottingham heard that a policewoman removed two record sleeves of the groups' new LP — Never Mind The Bollocks . . . Here's The Sex Pistols — from Seale's shop window.

Bus inspector Charles Whit-

bread complained to police when he spotted more of the sleeves two days later.

Magistrates' chairman Mr Douglas Betts told 25-year-old Seale: "Much as we deplore the vulgar exploitation of the worst instincts of human nature for commercial profit, we must reluctantly find you not guilty."

Similar charges were dropped against Richard Branson, whose Virgin Records company produced the record and sell it in their 350 shops.

Mr Betts and two women colleagues on the bench were given the origins and definitions of the word by university professor James Kinsley.

Professor Kinsley, an Anglican priest and head of the English Department at Nottingham University said the word appeared in almost every language in one form or another.

STONES

He told the court that the word was common in Scandinavian and Germanic languages and meant a small ball.

It appeared in medieval Bibles but had been changed to stones by later translators.

In the 19th Century, said the professor, the word had become vulgar — but that did not mean rude. It meant it had become popular and was used colloquially.

And he added: "It meant and means that

Continued on Page Two

If they're in the news, they're in The Sun

LOVERS IN A WORLD OF THEIR OWN
PAGE 5

Bolan's girl may face crash charge
GE 11

GOODIES GET THE ROYAL HEAVE-HO
PAGE 7

Pistols mov is ON agai

MARCH TOUR PLANNE

THE SEX PISTOLS' full length feature film is back on again, and is scheduled to go into production in a fortnight's time. The movie will keep the band fully occupied through December and January, and it's understood that plans are being laid for the Pistols to headline a concert tour in March.

The film was called off two weeks ago, when one of the financial backers withdrew and U.S. director Russ Meyer returned home. In any case, costs had escalated, and it was developing into a big-budget picture — which was not what the Pistols' manager Malcolm McLaren had originally envisaged.

Now Meyer has been replaced by a new director, another backer has been found instead of 20th Century Fox, and large parts of the script have hastily been re-written. As a result, shooting is now set to start at the beginning of December. Marianne Faithfull remains as

leading lady, though it clear if the original title Killed Bambi?" will be

Dates are now being in for the Pistols' concer March, and several venues have already a book them, McLaren Cowbell Agency, who a up the tour, are citing ample of the recent Str tour which went off with barest minimum of troub

Commented a Pistols man: "We're still having lems with some venue councils, and the situatio helped by incidents like at The Clash's gig in B mouth (see story below some theatre manager coming round to our w thinking, and we expect t enough of these to enable put a tour together."

Meanwhile, three record managers have now summoned — under the cent Advertisements Act — displaying the Pistols' cu album cover in their windows.

Warner Bros. Signs Johnny Rotten & The Sex Pistols

Warner Bros. Records has signed the Sex Pistols to an exclusive long-term recording agreement for the United States and Canada. Warner Bros. expects to release the group's first album, "Never Mind the Bollocks, Here's the Sex Pistol," on or around November 10.

The album includes the A-sides of their four European singles—"Anarchy In The U.K.," "God Save the Queen," "Pretty Vacant" and the newly released "Holidays In The Sun."

Other tracks include "Liar," "No Feelings," "Problems," "Seventeen," "Bodies," "New York" and "EMI." The album was produced in England by Chris Thomas with Bill Price.

All of the Sex Pistols—Johnny Rotten (vocals), Paul Cook (drums), Steve Jones (guitar) and newest group member Sid Vicious (bass) contributed to the writing of the songs on the album. There are no immediate plans for any U.S. Appearances by the group as they are currently working on a film project with director Russ Meyer. It is expected that the film soundtrack will be the second Sex Pistils album on Warner Bros.

THE RICH KIDS (l-r) Glen matlock, Steve New, Midge Ure, Rusty Egan

Ex-Pistol re-signs to EMI

GLEN MATLOCK's Rich Kids have signed to EMI records. The former Sex Pistols bassist has completed the line-up of his new band and they have already recorded some songs, although nothing has been properly mixed and there are no record releases scheduled at present. The band's line-up has been completed by the addition of guitarist

Midge Ure who was formerly with Silk. The rest of the band is made up of Steve New guitar, and Rusty Egan drums. Live plans for the band are expected to be announced shortly.

Matlock and the Rich Kids were featured in SOUNDS September 3 issue.

2 WED   Sex Pistols fly to Luxembourg, probably for radio inteview.

5 SAT   Policewoman Julie Dawn Storey looks into the window of Virgin records shop in Nottingham and observes a copy of the Sex Pistols album with the title 'Never Mind The Bollocks'. She informs the store manager, Chris Searle that she believes the word 'Bollocks' contravenes the Indecent Advertising Act of 1899 and that he may be liable for prosecution. The title of the album had been suggested by Steve and Paul. They had got it from a mate (Simon?) who was a hot dog seller around Piccadilly who was always saying it.

The music papers announce that the Sex Pistols film (at that time called 'Who Killed Bambi' and including Marianne Faithfull) is being called off for a short period due to the budget increasing to £750,000 and one of the financial backers dropping out.

Music press announce the Rich Kids have signed to EMI records.

Full page advertisements appear in the music press for the Sex Pistols long awaited debut album 'Never Mind The Bollocks'. Melody Maker and Record Mirror censor the word "Bollocks". The papers also run reviews on the album. The album has been recorded at Wessex and AIR studios over a period between March and August 1977.

11 FRI   Johnny Rotten takes his driving test – and fails!

12 SAT   All over the country the Sex Pistols album title is causing uproar as the Police respond to complaints about shop window displays and posters. Many shops are warned that they could be prosecuted under a 1899 law regarding obscene advertising!

17 THUR   The Sex Pistols start a tour of radio stations and personal appearances at branches of Virgin record stores. Today they appear at Virgin records in Nottingham, they then go to BBC Radio Nottingham and then on to Radio Trent. From here it's on to Virgin records in Sheffield and finishing at Radio Hallam.

18 FRI   Today's first visit is to Virgin records in Manchester, then it's on to Piccadilly Radio followed by BBC Radio Manchester. On to Liverpool and the local Virgin record shop. After this they visit Radio City and BBC Radio Merseyside.

19 SAT   Today it's Glasgow. Virgin records, Radio Clyde, then a drive to Edinburgh and Radio Forth. Finally a drive down to Newcastle upon Tyne and a visit to Metro Radio at midnight.

The music papers announce the Sex Pistols film is 'ON' again! Original producer Russ Meyer has been replaced and a new financial backer added. Plans for a major UK tour in March 1978 are also mentioned.

EVENTS WHERE EXACT DATE IS UNKNOWN:

Sex Pistols sign to Warner Brothers records for the USA.

NEVER MIND THE BANS

MARCH TOUR 78

SEX PISTOLS WILL PLAY

DECEMBER TOUR 77

Tickets: £1.75
If you are charged more DEMAND a refund

<u>1 THUR</u>   The Sun (newspaper) has a front page story "Sex Pistol and Girl In Drugs Probe". It goes on to describe that Sid Vicious and his girlfriend Nancy Spungen, have been arrested in a drugs probe. No charges were brought, pending the analysis of seized substances!

Glitterbest attempt to 'kidnap' Nancy Spungen and send her back to New York, but the plan fails.

<u>5 MON</u>   Sex Pistols play Rotterdam in Holland, Eksit club. Opening song: 'God Save The Queen' followed by 'every' song the band has ever recorded (barring 'Did You No Wrong') including 'Flowers Of Romance' and 'Belsen Was A Gas' and ending with 'Anarchy In The UK'. According to Sid Vicious, it is the best gig the Sex Pistols have ever played!

<u>6 TUES</u>   Maastricht, Holland.

<u>7 WED</u>   Tilburg, Holland. Pozjet club.

<u>8 THUR</u>   Arnhem, Holland. Stokuishal.

<u>9 FRI</u>   Eindhoven, Holland. De Effenaar.

<u>10 SAT</u>   Groningen, Holland. Huize Maas. Songs performed: 'God Save The Queen'/'I Wanna Be Me'/'Seventeen'/'New York'/'EMI'/ 'Belsen Was A Gas'/'Holidays In The Sun'/'No Feelings'/'Problems'/ 'Pretty Vacant'/'Anarchy In The UK'/'No Fun'/'Liar'/'Submission' (**).

<u>11 SUN</u>   Maasbree near Venlo, Holland, Maf Centrum. Songs performed: 'God Save The Queen'/'I Wanna Be Me'/'Seventeen'/'New York' /'EMI'/'Bodies'/'Belsen Was A Gas'/'Holidays In The Sun'/'No Feelings'/ 'Problems'/'Pretty Vacant'/'Anarchy In The UK'/'No Fun'/'Liar' (**).

<u>12 MON</u>   Day off from touring.

<u>13 TUES</u>   Wimschoten, Holland. De Klinker.

Pistols are denied work permits for Finland. They were planning to play a few concerts there in March 1978.

<u>14 WED</u>   Rotterdam in Holland. Eksit club.

Rich Kids play Wolverhampton, Lafayettes. Their 1st UK tour. Admission prices are pegged to a maximum of £1 and in some cases as low as 50p.

<u>15 THUR</u>   Sex Pistols return to UK.

Norwich, St. Andrews Hall – planned but not played.

Rich Kids play Coventry, Mr. Georges.

16 FRI   Sex Pistols play Uxbridge, Brunel University. The band appear on stage with the opening speech from Johnny "Welcome to the most dis-organised gig I've ever been to, I'd like to apologise, I'll get the cunt responsible". Songs performed: 'God Save The Queen'/'I Wanna Be Me'/'Seventeen'/'New York'/'EMI'/'Bodies'/'Belsen Was A Gas'/'Holidays In The Sun'/'Submission'/'No Feelings'/'Problems'/'Pretty Vacant'/'Anarchy In The UK'/'No Fun'/'Liar'/'God Save The Queen' (**). It is rumoured that the set was videoed by a member of the audience.

Rich Kids play Birmingham, Barbarella's.

17 SAT   Sex Pistols play Coventry, Mr. George's but Johnny's voice is bad due to having caught flu. Songs performed:'Seventeen'/'New York'/'EMI'/'Bodies'/'Belsen Was A Gas'/'Holidays In The Sun'/'Anarchy In The UK'/'Pretty Vacant' (**).

Rich Kids play Liverpool, Erics.

New Musical Express includes a 2½ page interview/article on Sid Vicious.

New Musical Express Readers Poll includes: Best Group - Sex Pistols (1), Led Zeppelin (2). Male Singer - Johnny Rotten (2), Best Album - Never Mind The Bollocks (1), Best Single - God Save The Queen (1), Anarchy In The UK (2), Pretty Vacant (6), Guitarist - Steve Jones (2), Bass Guitarist - Sid Vicious (6), Drums - Paul Cook (1), Most Wonderful Human Being - Johnny Rotten (1).

18 SUN   Sex Pistols planned gig in Wolverhampton, Lafayettes is cancelled because Johnny has flu and it is affecting his voice. It is re-scheduled and played the following Wednesday.

Rich Kids play Manchester, Electric Circus.

19 MON   Sex Pistols play Keighley, Nikkers club. Songs performed: 'God Save The Queen'/'I Wanna Be Me'/'Seventeen'/'New York'/'EMI'/'Bodies'/'Belsen Was A Gas'/'Holidays In The Sun'/'No Feelings'/'Problems'/'Pretty Vacant'/'Anarchy In The UK'/'No Fun' (**).

Rich Kids play Dewsbury, Mr. Pickwicks.

20 TUES   Sex Pistols planned gig at Birkenhead, Hamilton club is cancelled because of alleged "Police pressure on the promoter".

Rich Kids play Huddersfield, Ivanhoe's club.

21 WED   Sex Pistols proposed gig at Bristol, Bamboo club is cancelled because of a mystery fire that happened on Sunday (18th). So the band play Wolverhampton, Lafayettes club instead.

22 THUR   The planned gig at Rochdale, Champness Hall is cancelled due to local council pressure.

Long shot date for Pistols

By DENIS KILCOMMONS

THE Sex Pistols, Britain's most controversial punk rock band, are booked to appear in Huddersfield on Christmas Day.

In a stormy career the band have been sacked by a major recording company and had records banned by the BBC, including their version of God Save The Queen. They have won a court case over the title of their latest album.

The Huddersfield date will be one of less than a dozen appearances they will make in a mini-tour of the country after returning from concerts in Holland.

They are booked at Ivanhoe's which will have a 500 capacity for the night.

This is in keeping with the band's preference for playing small rock clubs rather than large concert halls.

Bill Wright, of Bankhouse Entertainments, who regularly books big name bands for Ivanhoe's Tuesday rock nights, said: "I know Christmas Day is a strange date but I am told this is the kind of crazy thing the Sex Pistols like to do."

John Jackson, of the Cowbell Agency in London, who handle the Sex Pistols, said: "I can't comment. Wait and see if the group play."

And his reluctance to confirm the booking is also in keeping with the way the band likes to appear at venues virtually unannounced.

Bill Wright added: "As far as I am concerned the booking is firm. Our regular Tuesday night attenders will be given priority over buying tickets for the Pistols."

The band are booked to play another Yorkshire date as well as Huddersfield, and should appear at Keighley's Knickers Club on December 19.

Pistols' party for firemen's children

CHILDREN of striking Huddersfield area firemen and laid-off workers from David Brown Gears are in for a Christmas Day treat from the controversial punk rock band, the Sex Pistols.

A bumper party for children under fourteen will now be an even bigger romp than originally planned, with invitations going out to more than 500 youngsters.

Sons and daughters of West Yorkshire firemen and of engineering workers from Brown's Park Works at Lockwood will join children of one-parent families at the party at Ivanhoe's, Manchester Road, on Christmas afternoon.

The Pistols have hired three buses to pick up children and take them to the party, where they will be greeted by 1,000 bottles of pop, a monster cake which will provide slices for all the partygoers, presents and a mountain of sweets.

Rudy Van Egmond, a representative of Virgin Records, who are helping the Pistols with the party arrangements, will be accompanied by his fiancee, singer Catherine Howe, whose parents live in Huddersfield.

23 FRI   Sex Pistols play Newport in Shropshire, Stowaway club. Songs
          performed: 'God Save The Queen'/'I Wanna Be Me'/'Seventeen'/
'New York'/'EMI'/'Bodies'/'Belsen Was A Gas'/'Holidays In The Sun'/'No
Feelings'/'Problems'/'Pretty Vacant'/'Anarchy In The UK'/'No Fun'/
'Submission'/'Liar' (**).

24 SAT   Sex Pistols play Cromer, Links Pavilion. Songs performed:
          'God Save The Queen'/'I Wanna Be Me'/'Seventeen'/'New York'
/'EMI'/'Bodies'/'Submission'/'Belsen Was A Gas'/'Holidays In The Sun'/
'No Feelings'/'Problems'/'Pretty Vacant'/'Anarchy In The UK'. (**). +
'No Fun'?

25 SUN   Sex Pistols play a Christmas party at Huddersfield, Ivanhoe's
          club. This is their last ever British gig, The event is in aid
of a children's charity and the children of local Firemen. They give a
free afternoon party and performance for 250+ local children aged under
14. This performance includes Sid Vicious doing versions of 'Born To
Lose' and 'Chinese Rocks'. Leftover turkey sandwiches are later given
out to fans queuing for the evening performance. In the evening the band
play for 1 hour 20 minutes (17 songs) 'God Save The Queen'/'I Wanna Be
Me'/'Seventeen'/'New York'/'EMI'/'Belsen Was A Gas'/'Bodies'/'Holidays
In The Sun'/'No Feelings'/'Problems'/'Pretty Vacant'/'Anarchy In The
UK'/'No Fun'/'Liar'/'Belsen Was A Gas'/'Submission'/'God Save The
Queen' (**). The gig is also recorded on the mixing desk by the sound
man 'Boogie' and Julian Temple is believed to have filmed it.

26 MON   A London Boxing Day gig was planned at one time. The
          possible venues included: The Lyceum, The Other Cinema
          (too small) and Croydon, Greyhound. None of these took place.

29 THUR   There are hassles over the Sex Pistols visas for the USA
          because of their criminal convictions.

31 SAT   The Ramones, the Lous, Generation X plus the Rezillos play
          London, The Rainbow. Sid Vicious fights with the singer of
          the Lous (a French band).

EVENTS WHERE EXACT DATE IS UNKNOWN:

One of the gigs in Holland (venue/date unknown) had the following songs
    performed: 'God Save The Queen'/'I Wanna Be Me'/'Seventeen'/'New
    York'/'EMI'/'Bodies'/'Belsen Was A Gas'/'Holidays In The Sun'/
    'Problems'/'Pretty Vacant'/'Anarchy In The UK'/'No Fun' (**).

4 songs from the concert at Maasbree (11th) are broadcast on Dutch
    radio. The songs: 'Pretty Vacant'/'Anarchy In The UK'/'No Fun'/
    'Liar'.

An interview with Paul Cook and Steve Jones is broadcast on Dutch radio.

A gig at Swindon (UK) is planned but never played.

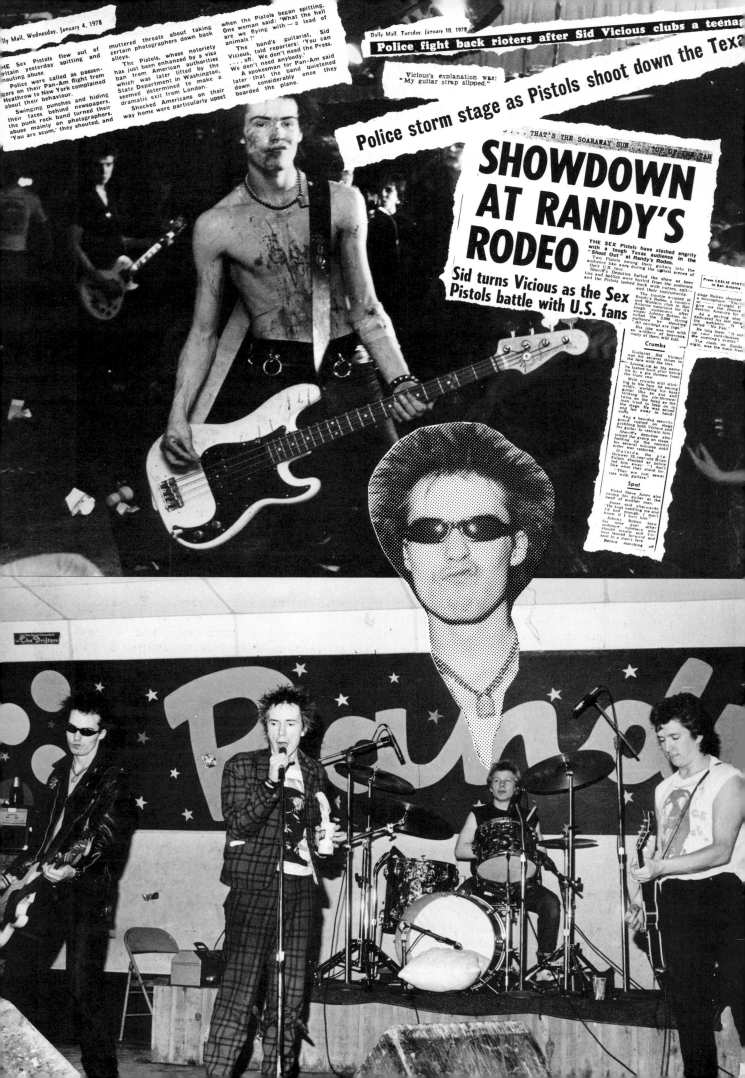

Daily Mail, Wednesday, January 4, 1978

THE Sex Pistols flew out of Britain yesterday spitting and shouting abuse.

Police were called as passengers on their Pan-Am flight from Heathrow to New York complained about their behaviour.

Swinging punches and hiding their faces behind newspapers, the punk rock band turned their abuse mainly on photographers. 'You are scum,' they shouted, and muttered threats about taking certain photographers down back alleys.

The Pistols, whose notoriety has just been enhanced by a visa ban from American authorities which was later lifted by the State Department in Washington, seemed determined to make a dramatic exit from London.

Shocked Americans on their way home were particularly upset when the Pistols began spitting. One woman said: 'What the hell are we flying with — a load of animals?'

The band's guitarist, Sid Vicious, told reporters: 'You can .....off. We don't need the Press. We don't need anybody.'

A spokesman for Pan-Am said later that the band quietened down considerably once they boarded the plane.

Daily Mail, Tuesday, January 10, 1978

Police fight back rioters after Sid Vicious clubs a teenag

Vicious's explanation was: "My guitar strap slipped."

Police storm stage as Pistols shoot down the Texa

THAT'S THE SOARAWAY SUN   TOP OF THE TA

SHOWDOWN AT RANDY'S RODEO

Sid turns Vicious as the Sex Pistols battle with U.S. fans

THE SEX Pistols have clashed angrily with a tough Texas audience in the "Shoot Out" at Randy's Rodeo.

Two Pistols swung their guitars into the audience like axes during the ugliest scenes of their U.S. tour.

Sheriff's Deputies halted the show as beer tins and bottles were hurled from the audience and the Pistols lashed back with curses, spit and their instruments.

The trouble erupted at Randy's Rodeo, a country and Western club in San Antonio notorious for it's tough customers, after singer Johnny Rotten insulted the 2,000 strong audience.

"All cowboys are just big girls," shouting.

His jibe was met with an artillery of beercans, many of them still full.

From LESLIE HINT in San Antonio

stage Rotten shouted a microphone: "You straight. If give me the chan destroy America for

As a parting shot dedicated his last song the audience called "No Fan."

He told them. "It sur up your contribution the evening's events."

The clash on Sunda night was the main from

Crumbs

Guitarist Sid Vicious was hit several times in the face with his name.

Lining-up to his bass he lashed back after being hit by a pie thrown from the front row.

With crumbs still sticking to his face he swung wildly, wielding his bass guitar like an axe and striking the pie-thrower twice on the head as the man tried to leap on to the stage. He was seized and led away in hand-cuffs.

And a bearded security guard rushed on stage grabbing both Vicious and his guitar to restrain him.

Sheriff's deputies also joined the group on stage, holding up the concert for several minutes until order was restored.

Outside, the pie-thrower 32-year-old Brian Fulpin shouted as police led him away: "I don't like what they stand for."

"They are just sewer rats with guitars."

Spot

Pistol Steve Jones also swung his guitar at the heart of another man.

Jones said afterwards: "He kept needling me and I'd had enough. I don't know if I hurt him.

Johnny Rotten blew his nose over other audience and other band members who should insult and Vicious leaned forward and spat in a man's face.

Before marching off

1 SUN   London Weekend Television screen a special 45 minute documentary 'The Year Of The Punk' presented by Janet Street-Porter and including interviews with Johnny Rotten and Dee Generate of Eater plus a performance by Siouxsie & the Banshees.

3 TUES   Sex Pistols fly out to the USA to start what was originally a proposed 19 day tour. They are met by Warner Bros. (their American Record company) who take over 'looking after the band'.

5 THUR   Sex Pistols first concert in the USA takes place at Atlanta, Georgia, The Great Southeast Music Hall. About 600 people turn up plus 5 TV crews, 30 photographers and 20 critics. Johnny opens up the concert with the words: "Hullo my name's John and this is the Sex Pistols". Songs performed: 'God Save The Queen'/'I Wanna Be Me'/'Seventeen'/'New York'/'Bodies'/'Submission'/'Holidays In The Sun'/'EMI'/'No Feelings'/'Problems'/'Pretty Vacant'/'Anarchy In The USA' (**). The band later agree that it was one of their worst ever performances and admit they have played badly. Johnny sings flat, Steve's guitar is out of tune and the timing is erratic. They do not play an encore.

6 FRI   Sex Pistols play Memphis, Taliesyn Ballroom. Songs performed: God Save The Queen'/'I Wanna Be Me'/'Seventeen'/'New York'/ 'EMI'/'Bodies'/'Belsen Was A Gas'/'Submission'/'Holidays In The Sun'/'No Feelings'/'Problems'/'Pretty Vacant'/'Anarchy In The USA'/'No Fun' (**).

7 SAT   The Sex Pistols are in Memphis holding a press conference.

8 SUN   Sex Pistols play their 3rd US concert at San Antonio, Texas. Randy's Rodeo, where Sid Vicious smashes his guitar over the head of a member of the audience who tries to get onto the stage and Johnny is quoted as saying "Oh dear, Sidney seems to have dropped his guitar". The show is then held up for about 10 minutes. Quotes from Sid include "You Cowboys are all faggots" and "That (beer) can hit me right in the mouth. It hurt but I don't care". About 2200 people attend this sold out concert. Songs performed: 'God Save The Queen'/'I Wanna Be Me' /'Seventeen'/'New York'/'EMI'/'Holidays In The Sun'/'Bodies'/'Belsen Was A Gas'/'Submission'/'No Feelings'/'Problems'/'Pretty Vacant'/'Anarchy In The USA' (**). Rumour has it that the show has been videoed by a member of the audience?

> Police with guns and small C.S. gas cannisters rushed on to the stage as members of the group's entourage held back Vicious.

Rich Kids play Glasgow, Satellite City.

9 MON   Sex Pistols play Baton Rouge, Kingfish Club. The audience start to throw coins at the band and following a request from Sid they throw dollar bills. The band pocket the money. Johnny makes 30 dollars. After the gig, Sid gets a blow job in the gents from a good looking female groupie. Songs performed: 'God Save The Queen'/'I Wanna Be Me'/'Seventeen'/'New York'/'EMI'/'Bodies'/'Belsen Was A Gas'/'Submission'/'Holidays In The Sun'/'No Feelings'/'Problems'/'Pretty Vacant'/ 'Anarchy In The USA'/'No Fun'/'Liar' (**). This show is rumoured to have been videoed on Sony Professional by a member of the audience.

Rich Kids play Edinburgh, Tiffany's.

The Pistols' parting shot

THE KSAN INTERVIEW with Bonnie Simmons — 14.1.78

RICH KIDS
(Matlock)
Produced By Mick Ronson

EMI 2738A

EMI 2738
0 6599

Rich Kids
©1978 EMI RECORDS LTD
ALL RIGHTS OF THE PRODUCER AND OF THE OWNER OF THE RECORDED WORK
RESERVED. UNAUTHORISED PUBLIC PERFORMANCE, BROADCASTING AND
COPYING OF THIS RECORD PROHIBITED. MADE IN GT. BRITAIN

SEX PISTOLS

JAN 14 1978

0211

**BILL GRAHAM PRESENTS
AT WINTERLAND**
8:00 P.M.
WINTERLAND
POST & STEINER STS. – SAN FRANCISCO
**GENERAL ADMISSION
$5.00**
NO REFUNDS – NO EXCHANGES

H.S. CROCKER CO., INC. S.F.

0211
GENERAL ADMISSION
WINTERLAND – S.F.

10 TUES   Sex Pistols appear on American national TV for the first time, a programme called Variety '77.

Rich Kids play Aberdeen, Fusion Ballroom.

Sex Pistols play Dallas, Longhorn Ballroom. In the sound check, they rehearse a new song called 'Sod In Heaven' (written by Jones & Rotten). A punkette from L.A. gives Sid a bloody nose as the band play on stage. Sid is so out of it that he plays with three busted guitar strings (and the bass guitar only has four to start with). This is their 5th US concert. Songs performed: 'God Save The Queen'/'I Wanna Be Me'/'Seventeen'/'New York'/'EMI'/'Bodies'/'Belsen Was A Gas'/'Holidays In The Sun'/'No Feelings'/'Problems'/'Pretty Vacant'/'Anarchy In The UK'/'No Fun' (**). The concert is broadcast on radio.

12 THUR   Sex Pistols play Tulsa, Cains Ballroom. It snows and Johnny, Steve and Malcolm all catch flu. In the sound check Steve and Paul play some old blues numbers and a version of 'Amazing Grace'. Sid finds a glamorous blonde with big tits. She later turns out to be a sex change! The show was probably taped and videoed by members of the audience.

Rich Kids plus The Accelerators play Manchester, Rafters.

13 FRI   Steve and Paul take part in a phone in show on Radio K-San in San Francisco.

Rich Kids debut single titled 'Rich Kids' is released on EMI. 1st 15,000 copies are in Red vinyl.

Rich Kids play Birmingham, Barbarella's.

14 SAT   Johnny and Sid take part in a phone in show for Radio K-San in San Francisco.

Rich Kids play Birmingham, Barbarella's (2nd night).

Record Mirror announces the results of its readers poll: Best Group 'T. Rex' with the Sex Pistols 4th and the Stranglers in 6th position. The Boomtown Rats top the Best New Artist/Band with Tom Robinson 2nd, The Stranglers 3rd, Elvis Costello 4th, The Jam 5th, The Sex Pistols 7th, The Motors 8th and The Damned in 9th position. Bore of the Year are the Sex Pistols.

Sex Pistols play San Francisco, Winterland Ballroom. 5000 tickets are sold in one day. Songs performed: 'God Save The Queen'/'I Wanna Be Me'/'Seventeen'/'New York'/'EMI'/'Belsen Was A Gas'/'Bodies'/'Holidays InThe Sun'/'Liar'/'No Feelings'/'Problems'/'Pretty Vacant'/'Anarchy In The UK' plus an encore of 'No Fun'. This is to be the Sex Pistols last ever concert. Johnny Rotten's last words onstage "Ah-Ha-Ha!! Ever Get The Feeling You've Been Cheated? Good Night".

16 MON   Sid Vicious O.D.'s and is admitted to Hospital.

Johnny Rotten 'given bullet'

SINGER Johnny Rotten has been fired by top punk rock group the Sex Pistols, it was reported from America this afternoon.

But a London spokesman for the band said: "This could be just one of many flare-ups.

"I won't believe it until I've spoken to manager Malcolm McLaren."

On the last day of their two-week American tour McLaren is Reported to have said that the Pistols will never play together again.

HIDEOUT

In Los Angeles the group was said to have decided to kick Rotten out because he was too destructive and was dragging the group down.

But Rotten, who has fled to a New York hideout says he is fed up of playing with the Pistols.

Their London spokesman said: "It it's true, then we will have to cancel shows in Sweden, Holland and Belgium.

"I'm not treating these reports too seriously yet—American tours are very arduous and this split could have happened because nerves are getting frayed."

Right before the Pistols went on that night Rotten said in the dressing room, "Le really fuck it up tonight. We'll fuck up these fucking hippies. We'll turn the table mates, and do something they haven't read about in the music press!"

Sid opened the concert with a few Ramones licks—"Basement" and "Blitzkrie Bop." It was all downhill from there. At one point the sound was so distorted all yo could hear was John's vocals and Paul's drums—the mikes were completely off.

"You can put up with anything," Rotten told the enthusiastic crowd. "There's no enough presents. These ain't good enough. Cameras? Do we have any cameras?

"Whoever hit me in the 'ead—it didn't hurt a bit, so tough shit!" Sid yelled, as usual as he got pelted with a few cans. During the show several guys fainted and had to be dragged out over the stage.

"I think it's fun. Do you want your ears blown out some more?" Johnny yelled after an especially bad song. The house lights came on. "Hey—the monitors are comple- tely off. Wait—they just came back on. This song is about you. It's called "Prob- lems"."

"One Two Three Four!!" shouted Sidney "Ramone" Vicious.

The song ended as Rotten was at it again. "Tell us what it's like to have bad taste."

Malcolm was extremely depressed after the show. "Fuckin' awful show, wasn't it? They were just like any other rock band." Everyone connected with the band felt the same way.

The Winterland security tried to throw Rory Johnson, the Sex Pistols' American Manager, out of the hall. "I'm the fucking manager of the group!" he hollered. The security tried to throw him out anyhow.

"Flower power fascists," muttered Malcolm. "Bloody fascists." He refused to go to the backstage party, he hates those things. Rolling Stone's Annie Liebowitz set up a bunch of lights and umbrellas at the party hoping to get a group shot for the cover. Rotten remarked to Joe Stevens—" 'Ere now, what do you think I would think if you and Bobby (Gruen) did all that?"

Joe Stevens: "You'd think we were over the top!"

Rotten: "Fuckin' right, mate, I'm not doin' it."

That night, two hundred Sex Pistols fans tried to sneak into the MiYako, where Steve Jones danced with Britt Eklund, Rod Stewarts old girlfriend. Did she spend the night with him? "She told me not to say anything," he said, "but use that bit in your story!"

The road crew took great pleasure in relating to me how they ignored McLaren's attempts at getting unknown punk bands onstage at the Winterland. They thought McLaren was a rank amateur who had no business being in rock and roll. They also considered him a security leak. "Winterland was the best show man. Graham sure knows how to put on a show!" Proof of this was that Bill Graham actually liked the music. The road crew didn't.

Rotten didn't want to go to Rio so he had Noel Monk book him into a hotel 25 miles away in San Jose. He was sick from the flu and had been throwing up blood. He was also tired of Malcolm's publicity stunts. He also hates flying.

Sid was stying with some punkettes in Haight-Ashbury, of all places. Noel figured that his job ended at Winterland, so if Sid killed himself at this point, it's not his fault.

At 6:00 A.M. on the 16th of January, Steve, Paul, Malcolm, and the rest of the Pistols staff piled into cabs and drove out to the airport to catch the flight to Rio. Malcolm drove out to John's hotel with Sid to talk him into going to Rio, but gave up on the whole mess. Everyone missed the flight, so they drove back to the MiYako. Paul and Steve hung around all day and were very depressed. Sid O.D.'d that day, in addition to passing out on the plane on the way to New York.

<u>17 TUES</u>   THE DAY THE SEX PISTOLS SPLIT UP<u>.</u>

Rich Kids play Keighley, Nikkers Club.

Paul and Steve tell Johnny that they've had enough and quit. They then fly to Rio de Janeiro in Brazil where a concert has been planned but never takes place.

THE END.

STEVE + PAUL RETURNING BY CAB FROM S.F. AIRPORT AFTER ABORTED TRIP TO RIO CANCELLED. THEIR DISPLEASURE WAS INSTRUMENTAL IN CAUSING THE BAND'S DEMISE.

STEVE AND PAUL WAIT FOR FLIGHT 515 TO RIO

↑JOHN WAITING FOR A FLIGHT TO N.Y.C. ↓Bleecker Rotten.

The next day, January 17th—John was in the MiYako hotel restaurant. Steve and Paul came over, hemmed and hawwed, sat down with Rotten. John said, "You've got to come out in the open some time."

"I want to leave the group," stated Paul.

Shortly after Paul and Steve told John that they quit, Rotten went up to Malcolm's room. Lying in the bed dressed in his underwear, McLaren told Rotten that the band was a "bunch of bleedin' cunts." and they were unmanageable, particularly Rotten. He wanted out, Steve wanted out, and Paul wanted out. He accused Rotten of being unavailable for talking about the Rio Gig. If John was not at his hotel and doesn't return his (McLaren's) calls, then WHAT IS IT?

Rotten's rebuttal was that he wasn't hiding from the band at all. His intentions weren't to conflict with the band and he would have gone to Rio if Steve or Paul had spoken to him about it.

McLaren said Bullshit. Rotten didn't return their calls and refused to go to Rio.

Rotten said he just didn't know about it.

McLaren accused Rotten of turning into Rod Stewart.

Rotten accused McLaren of trying to turn him into Rod Stewart.

ABOVE - J. ROTTEN WITH JODY BEACH OF THE ERASERS - HIS DATE. BELOW - ASSORTED SCUM-BAGS, RUFFIANS, PINHEADS + GEEKS GRAB MR. ROTTEN AS HE EXTRICATES HIMSELF FROM "THE MAGNET" C.B.'s (All pix this page Joe Stevens)

"WHEN I COME TO AMERICA I'M GOING STRAIGHT TO THE GHETTO. AND IF I GET BULLSHIT FROM THE BLACKS IN NEW YORK I'LL JUST BE SURPRISED AT HOW DUMB THEY ARE. I'M NOT GOING TO HANG OUT WITH THE TRENDIES AT MAX'S AND THE C.B.G.B." -JOHNNY ROTTEN <u>ROLLING STONE</u> OCT. 20 1977

Paul Cook and Steve Jones used their tickets to Rio. They didn't go to jail.

Johnny Rotten flew to New York with Joe Stevens. He stayed at Joe's house, and spent most of the time hanging out with the trendies at CBGB's and Max's. He managed to alienate numerous people who tried to talk to him by being   obnoxious and cocky. He mentioned again that he hates punk rock and only likes reggae. He flew to Jamaica a few weeks later and cut what was reportedly a good reggae song.

Sid Vicious ended up in the hospital in Jamaica, Queens. He told us over the phone that he was very lonely because no one came to visit him. He also said that Johnny Rotten was finished as a performer and finished as a person. No way will the Sex Pistols ever get together again.